A BONA FIDE CONQUEROR

By Sharon Quarles

A Bona Fide Conqueror

A BONA FIDE CONQUEROR

A Bona Fide Conqueror

Copyright © 2021 by Sharon Quarles

All rights reserved. No part of this book may be reproduced, scanned, or distributed in any printed or electronic form or by any means without prior written consent of the author, except for brief quotes used in reviews. Please do not participate in or encourage piracy of copyrighted materials in violation of the author's rights. Purchase only authorized editions.

Published by
Hadassah's Crown Publishing, LLC
Simpsonville, SC

Library of Congress Catalog Number: 2021908124

ISBN 978-1-950894-50-5

Printed in the United States

Dedication

This book is dedicated to my LORD and Savior Jesus Christ who gave me the courage to share my life story. I dedicate this book to my loving husband, Neil. Thanks for believing in me and being by my side. I dedicate it to my daughter Briana and my son Dion. I love you. Thank you both for your support. I dedicate it to my sister who helped refresh my memory on some subject matters and encouraged me until the end. We are bona fide conquerors, Sis! I dedicate this book to my other siblings as well. I love you. I dedicate it to my parents. Despite it all, I love you. I dedicate this book to my mother-in-law Roxie; I love you dearly. I dedicate it to my aunt-in-law, Luellen. I can always depend on you. Lastly, I dedicate this book to anyone who has ever experienced sexual abuse. May this book give you HOPE. No matter how it may feel, you are a BONA FIDE CONQUEROR!

A Bona Fide Conqueror

A Bona Fide Conqueror

Contents

Chapter 1	In the Beginning	5
Chapter 2	The Move	10
Chapter 3	Lost Innocence	29
	"Daddy Daddy, Please Go Away"	60
Chapter 4	I Got Away	61
	"Everybody Needs Someone"	77
Chapter 5	Life After the Abuse	78
Chapter 6	The Set Up	92
Chapter 7	It Is Well With My Soul	97
Acknowledgements		114
About the Author		118

A Bona Fide Conqueror

Chapter 1
In the Beginning

Psalms 127:3 New Living Translation
Children are a gift from the LORD; they are a reward from Him.

It all began in a small, country town in South Carolina. My parents were married on April 22, 1963, and I came into the world on June 6, 1968. Several years thereafter, my parents had a house built in a predominantly black neighborhood atop a hill. We only had a glimpse of one neighbor's house from a distance. While the house was under construction, my parents rented a small-scale house to accommodate them, my five siblings, and me. Beforehand, my parents lived in a much roomier, rented house, but they had to move due to smoke damage.

The current rented house chiefly consisted of three rooms: a small bedroom, a front room, and a minuscule bathroom. Mama and Daddy (aka Deddy) slept on a double bed in the bedroom with my youngest brother, Roy. In the front room, my sister Janelle and I slept at the top of the double bed, while my brothers Richard, Wiley, and Donnie slept at the bottom. The bathroom consisted only of a toilet. We washed our hands at the spigot that was on the outside of the bathroom. We bathed in a galvanized tub that hung on the wall behind the black potbelly stove when it wasn't in use. The potbelly stove kept us warm on those frigid days and those bitterly cold nights. It also served as a station where mama prepared some of our meals. In addition, an electric stove helped with the meals.

Growing up, my siblings and I had babysitters quite often. As an adult, I asked Mama, "Why did we have so many babysitters growing up?"

"Ah, me and your daddy always hung around at Black's Cafe," she answered. Her response answered some other questions I had in the back of my mind. The majority of my siblings and I are what you typically know as *stair-step kids*. My brother Donnie was six, my sister Janelle was five, I was four and my brother Roy was three while we lived in the rented house. My brother Richard was eleven and my brother Wiley was nine. Believe it or not, they were part of the babysitter crew. It is a no-brainer to see that they should not have been our babysitters and needed a babysitter themselves.

One day while the stove was blazing with its fierce hot flames, I asked Wiley for a glass of milk. Within seconds, I found myself being thrust forward, which caused me to fall against the stove. I came up with charred skin alongside my arm and wrist. I do not recall every intricate detail of this incident, but what I do recall from the incident is ingrained in my memory. Apart from that, the scars forever remind me of that day.

The mishap I had on the stove is incomparable to

what Janelle experienced. Richard deliberately held her arm against the burning hot stove for several seconds, which probably felt like minutes to her. There was no justifiable reason for him doing this; it was purely done out of spite. When Mama returned to the house, he told her that Janelle had accidentally fallen on the stove. This is probably what Wiley told Mama about me as well.

 Instead of taking Janelle to the doctor, Mama applied some type of cream to the wound and coated it with Vaseline. She then affixed a brown paper bag over the wound and wrapped it with gauze. I questioned Mama and I even asked Deddy, "Did y'all take me to the doctor or bandage me up when I got burned on the stove?" Neither one could remember what the outcome was when I was burned. My burns may have been bandaged, but my guess would be that I didn't go to the doctor. Janelle also has a scar to remind her of her ordeal. We most likely had at least a second-degree burn, but thank God, He saw us through.

 Richard and Wiley were very devious and cunning. I genuinely had a fear of them, and so did my other siblings. They had a different father from the rest of us. I used to ponder on the last name difference, but it all unfolded when I became older. Their having a different father could have been a contributing factor to their callous acts toward us.

 We were only about two minutes away from Grandma Dorothea when we lived in the rented house. When we crossed to the other side of the road and walked down the narrow dirt road, we would then see her house on the sloped hill on the right. Grandma Dorothea was my mama's mom. She was a soft-spoken woman but always spoke up if she needed to. Grandma loved to sing in church. I can almost hear her singing these words from one of her favorite songs:

> *Be what you are and live the life.*
> *God knows your heart, you can't get by.*
> *He's coming back, to judge the world*
> *Be what you are and live the life.*

Grandma's husband died before I was born. I heard many stories of how mean of a man Grandpa was. I also heard he was a great singer. Singing does run in the family. I was told he was a hardworking man during the week, but a violent and obnoxious drunk on the weekend.

The one story that sticks out to me like a sore thumb is the one about the house cat. As usual, Grandpa came home drunk. The purring cat came up to Grandpa and rubbed up against his leg. Without hesitation, he grabbed the cat by its neck and ferociously threw it in the hot burning heater. Grandpa stood laughing hysterically, never flinching, as he watched the cat reduce to ashes. When my uncles, told the story, they said it was an agonizing sight to see and a horrible stench to smell.

It saddened me to learn of Grandpa battering Grandma. My uncles had gotten fed up with him beating on their mother and tried to take up for her. In this one episode when Grandpa was beating on

Grandma, Uncle Brodie grabbed a black, cast-iron skillet and gravely thrashed Grandpa over the head, causing him to blackout. Uncle Brodie and his brothers thought Grandpa was dead, so they immediately decided to run away. I can't recall if they ended up going back home or if Grandpa simply caught up with them. In any case, when they did cross paths, Uncle Brodie got a bloodthirsty beating from Grandpa like he had never gotten before.

Although Grandma was soft-spoken, as I already mentioned, I deemed her to be a strong woman. If I didn't hear the stories for myself, I would have never speculated that she was an abused woman. This is a prime example of why people should not be judged by how they act. Regardless of how it may look, people never precisely know what others go through or what they have endured. Grandma Dorothea was called to her eternal home on April 2, 1999.

Chapter 2
The Move

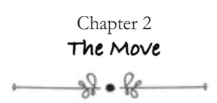

Isaiah 41:10 New Living Translation
Don't be afraid, for I am with you. Do not be dismayed, for I am your God. I will strengthen you. I will help you. I will uphold you with my victorious right hand.

Excitement filled the air as we packed to relocate to the new three-bedroom, one-bath brick house. The new house was relatively larger than the rented house. But being roughly 950 square feet, it was unquestionably compact for a family of eight. If only two people were in the kitchen, it felt cramped. But it had to make Mama happy just to have a kitchen.

Mama had Janelle cooking in the kitchen at the ripe age of nine. I most likely was exempt from the kitchen because I was the youngest, the youngest female that is. I reckoned Mama didn't think I was going to get married and have a family. Donnie and Roy always teased Janelle about her cooking. Donnie called her "Thelma" from the well-known black sitcom *Good Times*. Thelma's brothers, JJ and Michael, picked on her cooking and Donnie did the exact same thing to Janelle. Poor Janelle! She had to roll with the punches and tolerate the ridicule, but eventually, she became a great cook.

A Bona Fide Conqueror

Instead of overseeing Janelle in the kitchen, Mama engaged herself in other things, such as sewing, watching television, taking a nap, or maybe even leaving the house. Mama only took the time to show Janelle how to prepare a few dishes. Janelle basically had to attentively watch Mama in the kitchen to grasp recipes and techniques. This could have been a great bonding experience, but as usual, Mama didn't take advantage of it. For some obscure reason, Mama always had a closer bond with our brothers, which caused Janelle and me to have a deeper longing for her love and affection. I have questioned Mama on occasions, asking "Why weren't you there for me?"

Her answer never changed. She always replies, "Sharon, I didn't know how to be a Mama." I was in much disbelief, so I would rebound and say, "That's such a lame excuse." One time, I even went a little further by adding, "Being a good mother is a God-given or innate gift! You didn't show me how to be a good mother but I'm pretty darn good at it!"

Mama and Grandma Dorothea had a good solid relationship, so for her to use that excuse was a little sketchy to me. While Mama had a better relationship with my brothers, they too lacked the *complete* love and nurturing that they needed as children. Mama had the mentality of the older generations, that a woman's place was to stay home, cook, clean, and *"supposedly"* take care of the family. Maybe she had Janelle in the kitchen to prepare her for how she perceived things.

Despite Mama having that belief, every now and again she seized employment for a short stretch of time. The first place she worked was at a textile plant that didn't require a high school diploma or a college degree. Surprisingly, this is the place where I met my husband. Decades later, when the plant shut its doors forever, it upset and disheartened a lot of people. An unreasonable amount of the plant's employees who didn't have diplomas or college degrees had worked there for many years, relying on their jobs for survival.

I loved going to the big Christmas event this company hosted every year. There was an abundance of free food to choose from. We took complimentary photos with Santa Claus, and were able to sit on his lap and tell him what we wanted for Christmas. Each employee's children were given an oversized, red Christmas stocking stuffed with toys and candy. In the beginning, we could open our stockings right away. But when things got strenuous for Mama and Deddy, they held the stockings back until Christmas day. Mama and Deddy were able to purchase us a few gifts, nothing over the top, but with the Christmas stockings from the plant added, it appeared as if we received a slew of gifts. This kept us content. I very much looked forward to those events. Deddy started working there in 1976 shortly after Mama left, so luckily, we were able to continue going to the Christmas events.

I assumed Mama had to be a decent worker on her other job because she was able to work it sporadically. Meaning, she worked, let's say maybe a year, and then she quit. But it was no issue for her to turn right around and get rehired. She did this at least three times, I know.

This plant hosted a large Easter egg hunt annually.

When Mama was employed, we attended and we were thrilled to see the Easter Bunny. I enjoyed the Easter egg hunt, but I totally enjoyed the Christmas event better.

The stress of having a new house with new bills was probably what compelled Mama to find work from time to time. However, Janelle strongly believes that Mama was just being utterly slothful and negligent when she didn't work. When Janelle first said that I was like, "Wait a minute? Has Mama passed that trait on to me?" But after careful deliberation, I had to debate that assumption. I have been fortunate to have the opportunity to be a stay-at-home wife and mother for most of my married life. Before giving birth to my beautiful baby girl, I was a very devoted, hard-working employee. My husband, who was my boyfriend at the time, asked me if I wanted to quit my job and stay home to take care of our little girl. I gave that proposition much thought. At first, I was leaning towards saying, "No." I could not fathom that happening. Shoot, I loved to shop! Plus, I had gotten used to the idea of being an independent woman. My rationalization was that I didn't need anyone taking care of me. But what came out of his mouth next touched the core of my soul, and it sealed the deal.

"I don't want anyone else raising my daughter," he said in a solemn tone.

All at once, I felt gratitude in knowing that I was blessed with such a loving man who was willing and ready to take care of his family, and this was even before marriage! So yes, I quit my job. Adjustments had to be made, but I grew accustomed to them hastily.

I was able to spend quality time with my daughter. I read to her. I talked and sang to her. I taught her how to count and how to say the alphabet, even before she turned one. People were amazed. I mean, she did have her dad's smarts and was predestined to be smart anyway; however, I would like to think I played a small part in it.

I instilled good behavior in my daughter and reiterated to her that she was great and could do anything she put her mind to. I often took her to the library and to the park, even though she never liked getting dirty. I had the opportunity to do so much with her. It was such a gift from God! I knew what I craved as a child, so that made it twice as easy to convey that to her. I was able to attend all my daughter's school events. Mama never attended my events. I often volunteered at my daughter's school. Mama never volunteered for anything at my school. I went on most of her field trips. I can't remember Mama ever going on any of mine.

After I gave birth to my son four years later, I gave him that same attention. I also continued volunteering at my daughter's school. I just brought him along with me. He loved taking part in the activities, especially on field day! He also came along with me on most of the field trips. The teachers and principal loved my son, and they even knew him by name. They complimented me and were so impressed with how well-behaved he was. It was so gratifying hearing the compliments, and it made me feel very proud.

In the initial stage of living in the new house, we

had to get accustomed to some house rules. No matter how cold it was, we were in no way to ever touch the set thermostat. If we got cold, we just put on an extra layer of clothing. The thermostat was only for heat, and we had no air unit. Although we had a heating unit, kerosene heaters were mostly used. During the hot months, we set box fans in several windows.

Within a short time, a black rust stain had formed in the bathtub. When we took a bath, we were only allowed to run water to that mark. The water barely covered the heel of my feet! That act of inhumanity spawned me into overfilling my tub when I moved out on my own. When my children were old enough to prepare their own bath, I was unruffled as to how much water they ran. Thank goodness they never went to extremes.

I never knew what a showerhead was until many years later. We were just told not to touch it. Well actually, I thought it was to hold that funny-shaped bag that Mama used. That bag also had a nozzle and a long tube hooked to it. I didn't find out what that bag was until my latter years. A couple of my brother's friends spent the night at our house one time. They used the shower and Deddy nearly bit their heads off. They didn't know what they had done wrong. The only thing they knew was they took a shower. I felt sorry for them. I can imagine how embarrassed my brother was. Bless him!

My siblings and I had to be sure to turn off the light switch when we left a room. If we didn't, someone would have thought we committed a crime or something. We couldn't have a lot of electronics plugged in at once, not that we had a lot. Oh, and if there was a storm, everything had to be unplugged, and we all piled in the den with no lights on. There could be absolutely no talking.

When Donnie, Janelle, Roy, and I reached a certain age, Mama left us in charge of cleaning the house. Before that age, Richard and Wiley were responsible for cleaning. Instead of them cleaning, they assigned each of us a room to clean and checked after us to make sure it was done right. When Mama returned home, she would say "they" did a good job. Janelle and I were also responsible for washing the dishes. Needless to say, it was a heap-load of dishes for a family this large. Whew! I just had a flashback. I hate washing dishes even to this very day.

A few years after we got settled in our house, Aunt Jadie, Mama's sister, built a house next to ours, making us no longer the only house in that specific area. On the rear left side of Aunt Jadie's house was a large field. When we reached a certain age, we could play in that field.

We played different types of ball, which ultimately led us to start calling it *the ballfield*. We, several people from the neighborhood, and other surrounding residents, walked through that field so much that we created a path.

Walking through the ballfield allowed us to get to places a lot quicker. It only took us five minutes to get to Grandma Dorothea's house. A lot of times, Mama sent us to Grandma's to pick up sugar, milk, flour, or whatever else she needed, or we took Grandma whatever she needed. Mama had a lot of family members close by. When we stepped on the blacktop road leaving the ballfield, the first house we saw was the home of Mama's brother, Uncle Louie. As we continued the walk, we came to Cousin Juan's house. Grandma's dad and Cousin Juan's dad were brothers. Grandma's stepmom, Grandma Sella, lived just to the right of Cousin Juan.

The small path between Cousin Juan and Grandma Sella led us to Grandma Dorothea's house. Grandma Dorothea's sister lived right above her. Aunt Queena had a very, vicious dog named Big John. We always tried to walk without disturbing him. Well, we never succeeded. Big John barked and snarled at us vigorously. We had to run from him on many occasions when he broke free. I hated that dog with a passion.

One evening, Mama needed something, so she sent Janelle and me to Grandma Dorothea's to pick it up. She warned us to hurry because we had to go sing at a church revival that night. After we picked up the items we were sent for, we headed up the hill and saw that Big John had broken loose. He started to charge at us. We took off running with all our might. As I reached the path, I stumbled on a tree root and twisted my ankle. Even though I was in excruciating pain, I quickly jumped up and continued to run.

"Get back here, Big John!" Aunt Queena shouted. Thank goodness Aunt Queena called him back. That was the only way we were able to escape him.

After the chase, I told Janelle that I was in terrible pain. We stopped to look and saw that my ankle was severely swollen, and it was believed to have been a bone jabbing my skin. We somehow made it back to our house and tried to explain to Mama what had happened.

"Y'all, go in there and get dressed. We gonna be late!" she said fretfully.

Desperately trying to explain to Mama the pain I was in, I noticed she was not focused on what I had to say. She was more concerned about getting to church on time. I was taken aback when she demanded me to attend church without even examining my ankle. Holding back the tears, I coped with the pain. I could barely stand or walk. I literally had to drag my leg to get from point A to point B while trying not to attract attention.

When church dismissed, Mama still did not seem concerned about my ankle. The church was in the same neighborhood as our house. The pastor, his wife, and his two daughters, who were around my age, came for a short visit afterward.

I had planned to go straight to bed to get off my ankle. Any other time, I would have been thrilled to have company, especially since the company that usually came to our house didn't usually include kids of my age.

The first thing I did when I got to my room was to plop down on a clothes basket that was occupying a place on the floor. I tried to make the best out of the visit, but I was in *so* much pain. Even after the company left, neither Mama nor Deddy tended to my ankle. It was another situation I had to deal with on my own. I'm almost one hundred percent certain that

I had either a broken ankle or a sprained ankle. If I had to guess, I would say it was broken. I had to go to school in *so* much pain. I was pretty much invisible at school. No one paid much attention to me. Because I didn't have a doctor's excuse, I still had to participate in gym class. *OH, THE PAIN!* Unfortunately, I was forced to do other things that night with that pain. Thank You Jesus for being my Keeper!

One of our, *the stair-step kids,* favorite places to walk through the ballfield to was the corner store. In a sense of desperation, we searched for glass bottles, and once we accumulated enough, we took the bottles to the store and traded them in for money. Just as soon as we received the money, we hastily spent it in the store. We usually traded in enough bottles so that everyone could receive at least a dollar. With just that one dollar, we usually purchased a bag of chips, a candy bar, a bottled soda, and an array of one-cent candy pieces. Those were the good ol' days.

To get to the store, we had to go partially through the ballfield, and then we plowed through some trees and bushes. This route was a bit more rugged, but we lived for it. After plowing through, we waded through a water creek. Just as soon as we stepped up the small hill, we came to Uncle Larry's house. This was my mama's brother who we rarely saw sober.

As we continued walking up the graveled road, we soon came to Mama's sister's house. I have memories of Aunt Bae, but they are few because she died when I was fairly young. I do recall we were at her house following her death and my brother Donnie had stolen some cookies. Well, I decided I wanted to get in on the action. Donnie didn't get caught, but guess who did? When Aunt Sylvie, Mama's youngest sister, and one of my older cousins came into the room, I speedily stuffed the cookies down my top.

"What do you have chile?" asked Aunt Sylvie.

Of course, I answered, "Nothing."

But what did the cookies do? Plop, plop plop. The cookies fell from my top! I began to sniffle.

Aunt Jadie empathized with me. "Let that girl have those cookies."

I got to keep the cookies that didn't fall out, plus I was consoled with more!

I was about nine years old when we started walking to the store alone. Back then it was safe for younger children to walk by themselves. I mean, we had to be careful, but it was a lot safer than it is today. In my opinion, we still had no business walking that far alone at that age. We did not interact with Richard and Wiley, our older brothers, when we didn't have to. When they babysat us when we were younger, not that we were that much older at this age, we walked with them to different places.

Wiley, who thought he was a photographer, had us take pictures during the walks. He took shots with us high up in the trees or on the railroad tracks, and this was way before these types of pictures were in demand. We occasionally had good times with Richard and Wiley, but unfortunately, the bad times outweigh the good.

Richard and Wiley were teenagers, but they were not given the chance to live like teenagers. Instead, adult responsibilities, such as taking care of us, were flung to them. I'm sure this flustered them. Their anger and frustration must have built up and caused them to do things that had us utterly terrified of them.

Donnie, Roy, Janelle and I were verbally, sexually, and physically abused by them. When I say physically abused, I'm not simply talking about the expected sibling quarrels. I'm talking hardcore abuse. Richard and Wiley used numerous items to beat us. One of their favorite objects was the broken stove handle, which was easily removed and replaced. Another object often used was the thick leather whip Deddy used to *whoop* the boys. It seemed like the boys got *whoopings* all the time. Richard and Wiley also used drop cords, their hands, the broom, the mop, shoes, tree switches, or basically anything they thought could cause harm.

"Every time you don't touch the ceiling, you're gonna get a lick," Wiley scolded us.

Wiley used to urge us to jump up and touch the ceiling. Clearly, we got many licks because there was no way we were going to reach the ceiling. It must have given Wiley a rush to watch us strive to accomplish the task because we often had to attempt to do it. Richard just stood back and laughed.

Wiley was younger than Richard, but he, beyond a doubt, was the ringleader. Richard wasn't as underhanded as Wiley, but he most definitely played a part in the abuse.

"Give me my doll back! Give me my doll back!" I cried out to Richard. He kept pretending that he was about to return the doll to me. Richard kept this play up until he decided to grab me and tie me to a chair.

He kept teasing and belittling me. When I refused to kiss him as he had demanded, he repeatedly slapped my face. Richard finally decided to free me after I had been tied down for a lengthy period.

Richard and Wiley often made us pretend like we were getting married. Wiley liked to play the role of the minister. Whenever Janelle and I pretended to be the bride, they covered us with a white sheet used as our wedding dress. Curtain rings were used for wedding bands. This would have been an enjoyable enactment if Richard and Wiley didn't make us take off our clothes, pretending we were on our honeymoon. I remember always falling asleep though. Janelle and one of my brothers jolted my memory, telling me that this was not the only time sex acts were involved. It's been told to me by a counselor that a large number of memories have been repressed for me to stay sane. The stair-step kids had to rotate saving food from our plates to give to Richard and Wiley.

"Sharon, eat that chicken girl!"

"I don't want it, Mama," I said wistfully.

"Janelle, why you ain't eating that macaroni?"

"I don't want it, Mama."

"Roy, you not gonna eat your pie today?"

"No, ma'am," Roy answered gloomily.

We either secretly passed the food to Richard and Wiley under the table or we gave it to them when Mama and Deddy left the room. Really? Could they not have caught on to what was going on? I mean, with us repeatedly not wanting to eat the *main* part of dinner or with us not wanting to eat *dessert,* out of all things, shouldn't that have been a HUGE clue that something wasn't right? It doesn't seem like this would have been a strategy that they could easily keep up, but they managed.

We didn't tell Mama and Deddy about the abuse or about them taking our food from us because Richard and Wiley plainly let us know that if we told the beatings would become worse. The beatings were already brutal. They left many welts on us, so we didn't want them to be any worse.

At some point, Richard did not want to continue with the abuse. He probably started feeling guilty about it. Plus, it was also around the time he decided to live for the Lord. One day when Wiley was beating on Janelle, Richard kept telling him to leave her alone. Wiley continued hitting on her. When Richard stepped in to defend Janelle, they ended up getting into a fistfight. They also ended up breaking the right arm of the couch.

"Uhhhhh," was the sound Roy let roll off his lips.

WHAP!!! Richard forcibly struck Roy on his back, causing him to gasp. Richard wanted to do better, but at that moment he was provoked. Wiley slowly eased up on the abuse, but Richard ceased altogether. When Wiley saw that he was really in the game alone, he then receded completely.

I don't know if anything else happened that made Richard want to leave, but just as soon as he turned eighteen, he got out of dodge. He moved to another state and we didn't see him for years.

As we grew older, we filled Mama in about what we had endured from Richard and Wiley. She chuckled and said that she always thought we were in good hands with them. She probably thought that because every time she came home, we would be lined up on the couch not saying a word. Oh, the deceit!

By the time Richard had moved out, Mama had started settling down and was staying at home more. This was when she had given her life to God. Shortly before that, she had given birth to her last child, my brother Brandon, who is five years younger than me. Mama began cooking home-cooked meals every day. She loved to cook and frequently invited people over for dinner. If Mama did not do anything else, she made sure we were fed.

Many times, I saw her scraping up change for food and I often heard her say, "I don't know where our next meal will be coming from," but we always had a next meal. But God! I have even asked her, "How did you do that?"

By no means am I trying to compare Mama to Jesus, but some days it felt like when Jesus took those two fish and five loaves of bread! Well, you know the story. If not, this would be a great opportunity to read your Bible and get familiar with John 6:1-14. It is astonishing to look back and remember how Mama stretched ingredients to feed our family.

Normally during the week, Mama cooked one type of meat, two to three sides, bread, a dessert, and she usually made tea to drink. On Sundays, the meals were even more sumptuous.

I, too, love to cook. I delight in cooking meals for my family, and I find myself doing it in the same fashion as Mama used to do. I get excessive compliments on my food presentation and on the different types of food I prepare on any given day. I may have picked up my cooking techniques from Mama, but I cannot give her credit for my cooking expertise. I say that because Mama never showed me how to cook. I probably watched her subconsciously in the kitchen, but cooking is merely a God-given gift that I will remain grateful for, and I plan to always use it for His glory. I do need to give Mama props for showing me how to make some good cornbread, gravy, and tea. Of course, when I became older I had to do a little tweaking to make those my own.

I implemented simple tasks in the kitchen, but other than the cornbread and gravy, I did no cooking. Some of the simple tasks I performed were to batter and drop the chicken in the pan. Occasionally, I had to flip the chicken. I also picked out and discarded the remainder of the bad, dried beans, washed them, and put them on to cook. Oftentimes, I put food in the pressure cooker. I used to fear that thing in the beginning, but once I got used to it, I was fine. I'm sure there were a few other simple tasks I'd complete, but these are just typical examples. One other task that I would like to mention is greasing the bread pan. I despised it!

"Uggh, I hate lard!" I squealed as I became agitated with the icky, gunk between my fingers.

WHAM!!! Out of nowhere, I felt a gust to the head, causing me to experience a brief blackness. I could have sworn I saw stars!

"Mama, she's talking about lard, not the LORD!" Janelle expressed in my defense.

A Bona Fide Conqueror

Under no circumstances were we allowed to blaspheme or play around with the Lord. Nevertheless, I was left baffled when Mama didn't understand what I was referring to, especially since she was near to see what I was doing.

Church, besides the abuse, was pretty much my life and the only thing I knew. On second and fourth Sundays, Mama piled us in her burgundy station wagon, and we headed to her family's church located in the mountains. It felt as if we drove for hours, but it only took about twenty minutes. I often got carsick going around the curves, but my siblings and I kept ourselves entertained as we were tossed to and fro'. Church service was supposed to start at eleven, but it rarely started on time. Also, the pastor's messages were long and drawn out, so we got out late compared to other churches.

Grrrrrr. I would sit in church with a roaring stomach, anxious to hear the *"Amen"* that followed on the heel of the benediction. Hearing it signified that it was time to go home to eat, after Mama walked around to converse with other people, that is. Mama usually cooked the night before or that morning before we left for church, so we usually ate directly afterward. The funny thing is that up to the present moment my stomach still anticipates an early Sunday meal.

Mama probably prepared those meals because she knew we had to go back to church. We pretty much attended two church services, if not three, every Sunday. When we didn't have another service to attend, we drove around visiting different families.

A Bona Fide Conqueror

Since we didn't go many places, this was very exhilarating for us.

If a revival occurred during the week, guess what? More than likely we attended. In those days, revivals were prevalent, so.... Our denomination was Baptist, but we also attended plenty of fire-baptized, Holy Ghost-filled, speaking in tongues church meetings. I'd witnessed demons being cast out. I'd heard tongues being interpreted. I'd heard many prophetic messages. I've heard many other "teachings" that aren't taught to a great extent.

Both my parents professed to be preachers. Although Mama gave her life to God before Deddy, he stepped in the pulpit before her. Before that, Mama used to regularly hound Deddy while he was over the toilet puking his guts out after he had overindulged in alcohol. The sight and utter confusion used to put me in a panic. Mama used to boldly stand up to Deddy, and she literally fought him at times. By and by, Deddy finally changed his life, but somehow Mama changed, too. Years later, Deddy became the pastor of two churches. During this era, most Baptist churches only had two services per month. If there was a fifth Sunday, we had to attend the boring union meeting, but the rest of the day usually was free. Sometimes we didn't even attend the union meeting and that would be another time that went go visiting.

On the first and third Sundays, we accompanied Deddy to his small church, which only had a handful of members. I so dreaded going to that church for reasons I care not to discuss. Second and fourth

Sundays were when we went with Mama to her church; therefore, Deddy went to his other church solo. I became a member of Mama's church and I also was baptized. I was young when I was baptized, and I didn't even understand the meaning of it.

Now that I have given EVERYTHING over to God and have fathomed the legitimate reason for the deed, my intention is to be baptized at the church where I have been a member for over twenty years. If it wasn't for Covid-19, I would have already done this. I love my Pastor and First Lady.

Chapter 3
Lost Innocence

Ephesians 6:4 New Living Translation
And now a word to you fathers. Don't make your children angry by the way you treat them. Rather, bring them up with the discipline and instruction approved by the Lord.

At last, I had finally become a teenager! I was thirteen and hadn't started my menstrual cycle, so I was considered a late bloomer. I didn't gain knowledge about my menstrual cycle from Mama, but from school. Truth be told, Mama didn't just withhold the facts about my menstrual cycle. She didn't convey any essential information I needed to know in life. I learned the important facts of personal hygiene, how to carry myself as a lady, how boys, or anyone for that matter, should treat me, about sexual intercourse, and the effects of drugs and alcohol from school. The only thing I heard from my parents concerning sex was, "You better not go out there and get yourself pregnant!"

I was raised in a Christian household and I can't even recall a time where Mama or Deddy told me the effects of drinking or doing drugs. They probably assumed that since I was in a Christian home there was no need for 'the talk' to be given. That was not a guarantee, but I thank the Lord for His protection and

A Bona Fide Conqueror

keeping me away from that miserable demon.

Three days after my thirteenth birthday, my wish came true. I got it! I got my period! I had been eagerly anticipating experiencing this phase of my life. Had not the school prepared me for this pivotal time in my life, I bet it would have totally freaked me out.

When I went to the bathroom and discovered the blood in my panties, I called for help. Mama and I still had a fragile connection, so I had no yearning to tell her.

"JANELLE!" I yelled out.

Quickly entering the bathroom, Janelle asked, "What's wrong?"

"I got my period," I responded with excitement, but also with a sense of nervousness.

"Did you tell Mama?" I shook my head. Janelle left to go get Mama. When Mama entered the bathroom, the first thing she did was try to pry my legs apart.

"Let me see," Mama shrieked with eagerness.

I tightened the squeeze trying to keep my legs together and I exclaimed, "No, you can't see! Why do you want to see?" To this very day, I don't understand why she wanted to see.

I glanced over at Janelle hoping she would give me some help. She stood in the doorway with a disgusted look on her face regarding what was taking place. After the scuffle when Mama had finally managed to carry out her mission, she just left. Yes, that's right. She pried my legs apart, looked, and left. She did not tell me what it was or what to do. Without saying one word, she just left.

"What should I do?" I asked Janelle. I was very

much caught off guard by her ghastly answer.

"You need to roll up a wad of tissue and use it as your pad."

I asked with much confusion, "You don't have pads?"

Janelle responded while shaking her head with despair, "I'll tell Mama I need pads, but she never buys them."

My happiness quickly began to diminish. Tissue is only capable of retaining but so much. As a result, I had some incidents. It was very uncomfortable and exasperating having to sit on that big lump that never stayed in place. I had to decide if I would risk being late for class by stopping by the bathroom to create a new tissue wad, or if I would go on to class and pray the blood did not seep through.

There were days when the blood seeped through my clothes. When that happened, if I had a jacket, I tied it around my waist, which was a cool trend back then. The other times when I didn't have a jacket and the blood seeped through, thank God it wasn't bad enough to cause me to be the laughingstock of the schoolyard.

Janelle had started her period when she was twelve. She was familiar with the procedure for a couple of years already when I had started mine. We did not know why Mama didn't buy us pads. The only thing we knew was we had to use tissue for a pad. This was not what I had been looking forward to. Why we were put through that I will never know.

One night, we made a pit stop at a grocery store on our way home from church. Janelle had a brilliant idea to ask Deddy if he would buy us a box of pads. Well, she came out of the store with one of those enormous boxes of pads. When I say we were on cloud nine, trust me, we were on cloud nine! We took turns holding that box not wanting to let it go. Who would have thought a box of pads would've been so soul stirring? I hate to admit, but I wasted a few of the pads by changing way too soon. I did not consider the future; I just went with the thrill of the moment.

Issues were usually ignored in our household. Why didn't we receive pads continuously there afterward? Did Deddy not question Mama about us not having any? When I became an adult in hopes of making things make sense, I always asked questions.

"Mama, why didn't you ever buy us pads?"

"I had to cut up rags when I started my cycle," she responded.

I understood that it was a different kind of struggle for black people back then. I really did. But this was not a valid reason for me.

"You didn't even tell us to do that!" I exclaimed. "When I first got my period, you forcefully pried my legs apart and then you left without even telling me what it was, nor what to do. You always fussed asking, 'Who used up all MY tissue?'"

It's incomprehensible why it didn't occur to Mama that we were using tissue to catch our blood flow. Okay, let's say she thought we were using cut-up rags. How were we supposed to know to do that? She didn't tell us to do that! I wish we would have thought to cut up some rags. It would have been way better than tissue paper! I was thirteen and Janelle was fourteen. We always had to figure out things on our own, but our young minds were not mature enough to grasp that concept. I believe that if we had used some of Mama's sewing cloth, there still would have been a fuss. Janelle and I used tissue as a pad until we were old enough to get a job.

Fortunately for us, there was a special program that catered to low-income families that allowed early adolescents to work during the summer. We stocked up on pads to prepare for the months to come. Well, in our young minds, stocking up would only be one or two boxes. That was a clever move on our behalf. Even so, we were more eager to buy ourselves clothes for the new school year. At this age, it was imperative to have new clothes for the new school year. If not, we most likely would have been ridiculed.

Before we started working the summer job, we wore mostly hand-me-downs that we received from Grandma Sella. Grandma Sella undeniably had a mean streak. Sad to say, but when she was mean to us, we dished it right back to her. We deserved a *whooping* for being so disrespectful. Please, Lord, forgive me for the disrespect. When we were on the path that led us to Grandma Dorothea's house, Grandma Sella was famous for squawking, "Get out my yard!" Most of the time we just kept walking as we laughed and mocked her. But sometimes, Grandma Sella stopped us and said, "You don't have to if you don't want to, but I got these bags of clothes you can pick through if you like. But you don't have to if you don't want to."

She said this every time she had clothes for us.

Occasionally, someone gave her bags of children's clothes. Grandma Sella didn't have kids, so she let us pick through them. If we *wanted* to, that is. Oh, trust me, we wanted to! It was like winning the lottery or something. Grandma Sella was mean, and we were mean right back, but we always looked forward to receiving those clothes. We were nice to her then.

Getting my period was an indication that I was becoming a woman. Being looked at as a young lady had me "feeling myself," as the older generation used to say. Deddy called me to his room. I was certain Mama had told him about my recent milestone.

"You are becoming a woman now. Do you want me to teach you the facts of life?" Deddy asked.

"Yes, sir!" I answered with blissful excitement.

I had envisioned Mama giving me this talk, but since I just wanted the talk, I said, "Yes" in a hurry. With his beady eyes and a sly grin on his face, Deddy asked, "You won't get mad and tell anyone if I touch you, will you?"

As I took a deep sigh, I shrugged my shoulders and gave him a disheartened smile. My mood swiftly changed. In my heart, I knew something wasn't right. Boy, the school didn't prepare me for this one. I left his room and went to lay across my bed.

"You won't get mad and tell, will you? You won't get mad and tell, will you?" Those words kept replaying in my head repeatedly. I could not shake that bad vibe I was feeling. I regretted ever saying, "Yes." I stepped back into Deddy's room.

"I changed my mind. I don't want you to teach me the facts of life."

A Bona Fide Conqueror

I still recall the hideous look on his face as he snarled, "You already said 'Yes,' and once you say 'Yes,' you can't change your mind!"

I hurried back to my room and laid back across my bed. Janelle wasn't in the room, so I had the freedom to lay there and modestly weep like a baby. My initial excitement was robustly replaced with anxiety. By no means did I look forward to this teaching.

A week later, I was in my room doing homework when I was summoned by Deddy.

"SHARON!"

As I walked into Deddy's room, I saw that no one else was in the other rooms. The only room I could not see in was the living room, but I knew it usually was empty if Deddy wasn't in there.

I stood in the open doorway.

"Yes, sir."

In a subtle tone of voice, he said, "It is time."

"Gulp!"

I took a hard swallow and then I let out a sigh of panic.

Maybe he won't touch me, I told myself.

I just didn't know what to expect. Deddy motioned for me to come sit beside him on the bed. I slowly walked over and seated myself beside him. As soon as I sat down, he reached over to fetch a black paperback book called *The Woman's Body*. Janelle had mail-ordered this book several months prior to get a greater understanding of her body. When Deddy saw it, he confiscated it and told her she didn't need it.

He began flipping through the book, showing me

illustrations of people in different sex positions. Deddy wasn't saying a word, which made the situation significantly more bizarre. My heart was briskly pumping, and when he reached over to rub his hands across my body my heart began to pump even faster. I released a sheepish giggle as my naive self was trying to make sense of what was going on.

"Relax," Deddy said as he slowly lowered me down onto the bed. Not knowing what to do, I kept looking up towards the ceiling. I heard a crinkly noise that caused me to look to find out what the ruckus was. What is he doing? I wondered.

I quickly looked away when I saw him putting something over his penis. I didn't want to see that! I wasn't supposed to see that! Mind you, I was only thirteen, so I was clueless as to what he was doing. Sex wasn't a life-or-death subject that had to be taught at such an early age during this time.

Deddy placed his sizable body on top of my frail, skeletal frame. I laid there in bewilderment as he blatantly inserted his penis inside my vagina. In an eerie kind of way, I felt something break free from me. I witnessed a very piece of my soul fade away. I wasn't aware of what it was back then, but now I know without a doubt that that something was my innocence. I laid motionless as I kept looking up towards the ceiling until the heinous act was over.

When it was over, Deddy performed a false show of emotion: "I'm sorry, Sharon. It won't happen again. I don't know what came over me. Please don't tell and get me in trouble. Let this be our secret."

Even at this age, I had an inkling that something

wasn't right, but obviously, I was too naive to realize what was happening. Deddy knew it was wrong, or he would not have told me to keep it a secret and not get him in trouble. Of course, I didn't want to get Deddy in trouble, so I told him that I would not tell. Apart from that, he was my dad. He was supposed to know what was best for me and protect me. Also, he was a man of God. A preacher man at that. He was supposed to do what was right.

I always heard Deddy and other preachers say, "God will forgive us for all of our sins." I believed that Deddy was sorry, and I believed it wasn't going to happen again, yet I felt this act was too much to bear. I heard Deddy and other preachers say, "God won't put more on you than you can bear."

So, I just tried to suck it up. I felt very sad and so alone. Deddy and the other preachers also said, "God will never leave you or forsake you."

This young girl had to wonder though, where was God while this was happening? Why did He even let it happen? I was traumatized, and I was confused.

"Go clean yourself up," Deddy told me.

I really didn't know what he meant by "go clean yourself up," so I just went to use the bathroom. I was in a daze as I walked to the bathroom to relieve myself. When I wiped, I saw blood on the tissue. It startled me because I knew it had not yet been twenty-eight days. It wasn't time for my period to recur. The blood wasn't from my cycle; it was from the breaking of my hymen.

Evidently, penetration wasn't involved with my brothers. I went back to my room and laid across my bed. As I laid there, I began to have an outpouring of emotions. I felt dirty. Guilty. Mad. Ashamed. Sad. Disgusted. Hurt. Scared. And Alone. That day changed my life forever.

Mama soon returned to the house. Although I stayed mostly in my room that day, she didn't check on me. When I did come out, I remained very quiet and withdrawn, but Mama never questioned my actions. Here I was in this big family, but I felt so alone.

Another summer morning had emerged. The sun poured through my window, but I had no desire to get up. It was summer, so I stayed in bed a lot longer than usual this morning. I did not want to be bothered.

When I finally got up, I just lounged around in my room for the rest of the day. Mama was not working then, so she was there. This was the second day I'd been moping around, but she still never came to check to see if anything was wrong with me. In one way, I was relieved because Deddy told me to keep it a secret. On the contrary, I wanted her to decipher what was wrong so that I could perhaps recover and maybe not feel so alone.

Just like Mama, Deddy was dispassionate about having a healthy, well-grounded relationship with his children. He avoided giving us quality time. I never really saw him giving Mama quality time. It was like he was for himself and nobody else. He made sure he was taken care of. Deddy was well-dressed and well-groomed, while the rest of the family was mediocre. He always drove a better car than Mom. He treated

A Bona Fide Conqueror

himself like royalty.

There were three central areas where you could be sure to find Deddy: his bedroom, the living room, or the front porch. He always prepared *or pretended* to prepare sermons in his bedroom. He had a wall calendar with many distinguishing marks. I often wondered about those marks, but I know the marks had to symbolize something that meant no good. If he wasn't preparing messages, he just lounged on the bed and watch television.

The living room most likely was his favorite spot, because that is where he spent a lot of his time. The living room was, to a degree, broken off from the rest of the rooms. It was kind of like his hideout spot. Deddy had a brown recliner that he always sat in. It was in the perfect spot to see at first sight who came through the front part of the house. He also watched or pretended to watch the TV that was in the den. The reason I say he may have pretended is because I truly believe he sat in his chair plotting his next move. Deddy's recliner was right beside the front door. That was the door we mainly used to enter the house. The first thing we usually saw when we came in was Deddy sitting in his recliner with his swollen feet propped up. That sight was beyond mystifying, but the swelling was a result of the thyroid disease from which he suffered.

We pretty much had to stay out of the living room. This was the room for company. Mama forbade us to touch the piano that was in there. We did sneak and bang on it at times. A few of my brothers were able to hit a note or two. If Mama had let them practice more, a couple of them could have made great strides with their skills.

The last spot Deddy utilized was the front porch. During the day, he usually sat in a chair that was near the living room window. At night, he sat on the bench at his weight station directly in front of the living room window. In my opinion, the weights were set up under false pretenses. I say that because I only saw him lifting them a few times and even then, I think he was lifting to be a show-off at that moment.

Deddy was supposedly a preacher man, but he wanted to be regarded as a macho man. He carried himself as if he was this strong, ruthless, you better not mess with me, man. I must admit, some folks were intimidated by him. Sometimes when my cousins or my classmates saw him, they whispered or told me later, "Your dad is mean!" He never really did anything; it was just the way he carried himself.

In actuality, Deddy was a nervous and paranoid man with a lot of anxiety. One night, I detected a gap in the curtains, which allowed me to get a glimpse inside the house. I didn't always see the gap; I only noticed it when I was outside at night. It was a little suspicious because Deddy always made sure everything was locked and closed. Again, he was paranoid!

While I was trying to still get over the dreadful night before, Deddy called me into the living room the following night.

"Will you scratch my scalp?" he asked me.

Deddy and Mama always had Janelle and me to scratch or grease their scalps, so for him to ask that was not out of the ordinary. The big issue was that it was late and everyone else was in bed. Well, everyone except Mama. When I went to gather the necessary tools, she was working at her sewing machine. I returned to the living room and started the process. There was no conversation; I was simply just doing the job. This was my first time alone with him since he raped me the night before, and it was a bit awkward.

Minutes later, Deddy began to rub his hand over the bottom portion of my body. Panic set in quickly. Oh my God! Is Deddy about to do again what he did to me last night? He promised me that he wouldn't do it again.

Whew! I breathed a sigh of relief when I heard someone walking toward the den. I knew he had to stop because whoever was walking our way would have been sure to see what he was doing if he continued. When Deddy heard someone walking up, he dropped his hand from my body and reached for his glass.

"Keep scratching," Deddy said in a low voice.

He rolled the ice around that was in the glass as if he was trying to get his drink colder. I'd noticed he always did that as a distraction. He kept rattling the ice occasionally, until Mama headed back to her room. Mama supposedly had gone to the kitchen to get her something to drink, or maybe she felt like something was wrong. I don't know because she never said anything.

Just as soon as Mama made it back to her room, Deddy proceeded with what he had started, but this time he reached down the front of my panties and inserted a finger or two in my vagina. I became weak in the knees and my hands grew numb. Deddy stood up and guided me in front of him. He then stood up and inserted his penis into me. I was afraid someone would walk in and see what was taking place. I wasn't responsible for what was going on, but I was afraid I would be the one who got in trouble.

After the disgusting act, Deddy basically repeated the same show as the night before. He apologized and said that it would not happen again. Guess what? It did happen again. It happened the next day, then the next day, and then the next. This had started happening basically every day. It happened when family members were away or if they were in the house. It didn't matter; he was getting it one way or the other. It happened in the living room. Because of its location, it happened there a lot. He was able to see if anybody came to the front of the house.

Deddy usually kept me up late just to do his dirt. I was very sleep deprived. I went to school a lot of times with three or four hours of sleep. A few times, as I passed him in the small hallway, he stopped me and inserted his penis into me. He would have on his red and black buffalo plaid robe going to the bathroom to take a bath. The only thing someone needed to do to see what was going on was open a door!

Oftentimes, it happened on the front porch at night. That's exactly what that peephole was for! Deddy laid me back on his weight bench or sometimes he would prop me up on top of him. The one close neighbor who moved into Aunt Janie's house after she moved away sometimes pulled up while Deddy was doing his sin. Even though it was unlikely for them to see what was going on due to the darkness and distance, I always prayed they would somehow see and get me out of the mess. It happened in Mama and Deddy's bedroom. The room that was supposed to be their oasis.

Usually, when Deddy performed these horrific acts on me, I mastered how to escape to that secret place in my head that made me feel safe and secure. It was as if I had gone to a different dimension. The only times, which was not that often, Deddy didn't molest me was when we had out-of-town guests staying with us or if he just flat out couldn't make it happen.

Deddy had a kidney operation that left a scar on his left side. He complained about it being sore and always asked Janelle and me to rub alcohol on it. It started out that Janelle rubbed it for about ten minutes, and then I rubbed it for about ten minutes. Deddy wore long pants, but he removed his shirt right before laying down. Mama was always in the room.

As time passed, Deddy started wanting us to rub alcohol and lotion on the scar, and he increased the time that he wanted us to do it. Deddy started wearing shorts instead of long pants. Mama was still in the room, until one night it changed. One night when a couple of my siblings were in the room as I was rubbing Deddy's *scar,* he jumped up and yelled, "It's too noisy! Grab that stuff Sharon and bring it in your room!"

The stuff he was referring to was the alcohol, the

lotion, and the sheet that he always laid on. I grabbed it and before leaving his room, Deddy declared, "Y'all better not bring all that racket in here either! Better yet, y'all stay outta here."

Deddy only had one goal and that was to get me in the room alone. I had been raped in most of the other rooms, but this was new. Was I about to be violated in the one area of the house where I felt the safest? My room! I started to rub the alcohol on his scar as usual, but he said, "Don't use alcohol. Rub the lotion all over my back."

I did what was requested for a good fifteen minutes, and he began bobbing his body up and down. Later, he turned to his side and put his fingers in my vagina. With the other hand, he pulled out his penis and started masturbating right in front of me. He continued until he ejaculated all over the sheet. I'm sure I had to look like a deer in headlights. I was embarrassed and felt sick to my stomach.

This total process lasted at least an hour. Afterward, Deddy told me to send Janelle in the room so she could rub his back. Mama was still at her sewing machine on this particular night when I went to tell Janelle. I was already in there for an hour. She didn't have questions? Janelle ended up staying just as long as I did. I had asked Deddy at one point if he was messing with Janelle, but he denied it. My question was if he wasn't doing to her what he was doing to me, why the heck did she stay in there that long? Hmm.

Janelle and I were forced to ask Deddy every night, "Deddy, do you want me to do your back?"

A Bona Fide Conqueror

Sometimes he answered right away, but sometimes we had to stand there for a long time awaiting his answer. Mama saw us standing there, but she never questioned it. She just went on her merry little way. She didn't even seem concerned about us having to go to school the next morning.

I knew why Deddy had *me* waiting so long. Well, I know now, but didn't know then. He was watching and waiting for that perfect moment to have the chance to perform his dirty deed. If Deddy claimed he wasn't doing to Janelle what he was doing to me, why did she have to stand there for so long? My young mind could not comprehend.

I really despised rubbing Deddy's back. And every day? Whoo chile! It all depended on where Mama was as to which room I had to rub Deddy's back in. Yes, in the beginning, Mama was always in the same room. But that was part of his enabling factors, just like when it was only supposedly about rubbing alcohol on the scar to ease the soreness. It was no longer about the scar. He wanted the lotion rubbed all over his back. Sometimes he rubbed lotion on his hand before he masturbated. Alcohol was out of the picture. Hmm, I wonder why? The sheet was hard from all the dried-up semen. I knew why the sheet was hard, but I often wondered what Janelle thought. One night she asked, "Why is this sheet so hard?" We snickered about it but never said anything else about it.

Mama was at her sewing machine when I went to retrieve the items to rub Deddy's back. Janelle was also in Mama's room at the time.

A Bona Fide Conqueror

"Ughhhh, I don't want to do Deddy's back!" I said sternly.

"Me either!" Janelle followed.

Mama, who was not helping the situation said as she continued to sew, "Ah, y'all know ya daddy like y'all rubbing his back."

"But Mama," I said, "We shouldn't be doing this. You're supposed to be doing it!"

Regardless of what I had said, Mama still insisted that we make Deddy happy. I grabbed the stuff and with Mama's encouragement, went to get my daily abuse.

Another time when one of my older cousins came to visit Mama, I gained a wee bit of hope when Mama and my cousin entered the room. I was thinking, Yes! Something is finally about to be done!

When my cousin saw what I was doing, she looked very much disturbed. As she was entering the room, she was talking and laughing, but just as soon as she witnessed me sitting on my parents' bed rubbing my daddy's back, she quickly became shell-shocked. She couldn't believe what she was seeing. The shock was written all over her face. Mama didn't appear to be bothered by it at all. I was embarrassed, but like I said, it gave me hope of getting out of the situation. However, the abuse continued. Like everyone else, my cousin kept it under the rug.

Penetration was the dominant act Deddy performed on me, but other acts were performed as well. He masturbated and ejaculated in front of me. He made me jerk him off. He performed oral sex on me and tried to make me perform it on him saying,

A Bona Fide Conqueror

"It ain't nothing but skin."

Deddy wrote me letters filled with sexual connotations. Wordings in the letter would be something like: *I want to suck your pus*y. I want to eat your cu*t. I want you to suck my co*k. I can't wait to fu*k you.* Deddy quizzed me to make sure I read the letter. I should not have heard that type of language at this age, especially not from my own Deddy!!! Deddy made me get rid of the letters a certain way. First, I had to run water over them. Next, I had to pulverize them into small pieces. Lastly, I had to wrap them in toilet paper and place them at the bottom of the trash can.

Since I was introduced to those words and knew how to use them, I tried to exploit them to gain popularity with some of my classmates. I thought knowing those types of words would make me one of the *cool* kids. I was drawn more to peers who were more like me: gentle, ordinary, and somewhat nerdy. When I pretended I did those acts, my peers were sickened by the way I was behaving, which made them shun me for a few days. I faced them, told them I was sorry, and told them that I had made everything up. It wasn't right away, but they finally started back talking to me. I didn't do those things, but those things were done to me. I couldn't tell my peers that though. It was Deddy's and my secret.

When I looked back over things that had taken place, it made me realize a few things. You see, I don't believe Deddy just decided to molest me out of the blue. It may have taken him months, it may have even taken him years, but this most likely had been his master plan for a while. Why did he have that condom when he first molested me? Mama had given birth to seven children, plus she had one miscarriage. Apparently, Deddy wasn't using them on her, but he was sure to use a condom on me every time. He made it a point not to get me pregnant. Having said that, one day I had become very nauseous. I was hugging the toilet as I was regurgitating.

"You betta not be pregnant!" Deddy nervously shouted at me.

As sick as I was, I was awestruck as to what I was hearing. Why the heck was he yelling at me like that? He knew if I was pregnant, it would have been nobody's baby but his. Well, it could have been one other person's, but that was highly unlikely. I only slept with that guy once, and he used a condom. I knew there was a slight chance, but still. I met this guy at church, and I had sex with him at church. Thank you, Lord, for your forgiveness! I thought I was so in love with that guy. He was much older than my little teenager self. This guy knew what to say to make me feel special to get what he wanted. I just could not see it then.

Any who, Mama and Deddy watched in suspense as I was alone on my knees hanging over the toilet puking my guts out. I knew Deddy's uneasiness came from him thinking he might have gotten his own daughter pregnant, but I couldn't quite understand why Mama was so anxious. Could it have possibly been for the same reason? *Hmm.* I think I may have had food poisoning, but I don't know. I never went to the doctor.

A Bona Fide Conqueror

The abuse ceased momentarily, but just as soon as my cycle came and left, the abuse came right back into play. Deddy was so exhilarated that I had gotten my period that he took me out for ice cream. Wow. What a celebration.

It wasn't until episodes like this that I received treats. I did not go to the doctor on a regular basis, but when I did go, guess who accompanied me? Yep, Deddy! Another orchestrated plan. He took me because he wanted to know everything that was being said. He wanted to know what I told the doctor and he wanted to know what the doctor told or asked me.

I had to have a CT scan because I was having bad headaches that began in middle school. After the procedure, the doctor sat me down and fervently asked me, "Has anyone ever touched you to make you feel uncomfortable?"

I wanted to scream out, "YES! YES! YES!" but fear gripped me. I could hear Deddy purposefully popping his nails in the background. When he did that, it was a warning to let me know that he was listening. It meant I better watch what I said and what I did. After the brief pause, the doctor chimed back in, "You can trust me. Has anyone ever touched you to make you feel uncomfortable?"

Oh, how I wanted to tell the doctor so badly. Finally, after hearing the continuous popping of the nails, I hesitantly shook my head. To this very day, I believe the doctor had a sneaky suspicion that something wasn't right. Again, these types of things were not as openly brought up like they are today. The doctor probably should have dismissed Deddy from the room, but knowing Deddy, he probably would have refused to leave. A deep sadness overtook me as I was walking back to the car. I was infuriated and kept beating myself up for not telling the truth. That could have been my way out! I kept telling myself.

"Thanks for not getting me in trouble," Deddy said with glee.

Deddy then took me for hot dogs at one of his favorite fast-food restaurants. Certain things had to happen for me to receive treats, but Janelle got them all the time for no reason in my opinion. I could not process that in my mind.

There she was being treated like a princess, while I was being molested and treated like the *black sheep*. That caused me to have strong animosity towards her. Other people had noticed the different treatment as well. I know this because I heard it being talked about. This continued throughout the years. Deddy knew what he was doing without a doubt.

Deddy and Janelle seemed like they had a good relationship, so that is why I boldly asked him one day, "Since you and Janelle are so close, why don't you mess with her instead of me?"

"Ah, you know Janelle is a blabbermouth. She will tell and get me in trouble," Deddy said.

I didn't really want this to happen to Janelle. I knew the pain and I didn't want that pain to be inflicted on anyone else, including my sister whom I did not like. I just wanted some clarification. Janelle did talk a lot and was rather rambunctious, while I was more on the quiet and shy side. I just left it at that.

By now, I was a high schooler, but that didn't make

it any easier to get out of the situation. Deddy was a master manipulator, and he had started making threats to me. He said that if I told anyone, he would be taken away and nobody would be there to take care of us. He also said my friends would laugh and make fun of me if that happened. He knew what to say, when to say it and how to say it. He had a way of making me believe anything he said was true, even when I knew it was a lie. He told me lies to transpose my reality.

Deddy had some health issues going on and he used them to his advantage. He told me on several occasions that he was doing things to me because he was sick and needed my help. He was sick alright! And he most definitely needed help, but not mine! He had the audacity to say that the doctor had told him, "Whoever you are getting your juice from, you need to keep getting it because it is making you better."

First, what doctor said that? Second, his telling me that made me feel obligated in a paradoxical type of way. Oh yes, his aim was to make me feel responsible.

I prayed many times that Deddy would die. Even though I was a bona fide fighter, in a bizarre type of way I felt like it was my responsibility to make him better. Deddy had a way of making me feel like it was my fault or made me feel like it would be my fault if *the secret* was discovered. I never thought that it was something I did to cause the abuse, but I did feel like it would be my fault if anything happened to him.

Deddy told me that he would hurt me or anyone else I told *the secret*. That was one of the main reasons I did not tell. I didn't want him hurting me. Well, at

A Bona Fide Conqueror

times, I did wish that he would kill me. That is how atrocious the torment was. I didn't have any stable people in my life, but I still didn't want him to hurt anyone. Deddy, for the most part, kept me isolated from everyone. Basically, I was only allowed to go to school and church. I didn't get to hang out with any of my classmates like a normal kid. I often heard peers making plans to go to the skating rink, the movies, school games, anything fun. Every now and again somebody might say, "You ought to come!" Yeah right. We knew that wasn't going to happen. My peers had picked up on how sheltered I was. It was so embarrassing.

I was only able to attend three, possibly four, football games during my entire high school term. Each time, it was a shock. Janelle had the privilege of driving us to the games. They were always home games that we could attend. We had to literally sit together. We didn't have the privilege to walk around with our friends like the other kids. We had to sit. Deddy wasn't there, so why didn't we walk around? It was because he had that much unhealthy control over us. Even when he wasn't around.

I became best friends with a girl named Shannon who had moved into the neighborhood. Wow! I could have a real friend. Since she lived in the neighborhood, Deddy was able to easily monitor the friendship. Deddy didn't let me go to her house that much, but she came to my house practically every day. Which brings me to the next threat. "If you don't give it to me, then I will get it from your friend."

Deddy always threatened me with this. I was

scared to tell Shannon the secret, but now I had to worry about protecting her from my daddy. I continued fighting him, but practically let him abuse me so that he would not bother Shannon. It is very hard to explain how I fought, but let it happen. Deddy more than likely would not have touched Shannon, but this was another way he forced me to fall into his trap. In other words, he used that tactic to make me keep feeling obligated. I felt trapped back then, but I now can identify why God placed Shannon in my life. He knew I needed her. Thank You, God, for placing Shannon in my life.

I was also blessed with another person God placed in my life, and her name is Mama Lois. I always saw this lady at church who had such long and pretty black hair. She had such a warm and welcoming spirit that drew my attention to her. She wasn't a member of the church I attended, but I saw her at other churches and she occasionally visited ours. When I saw her, I made sure I spoke to her and she willingly gave me a big hug. On this night I did something out of the ordinary.

I asked her, "Can you be my mama?"

She gave me a startled look and said, "I can't be your mama dear, but I can be your godmother. How does that sound?"

I didn't even know what a godmother was, but it had "mother" in it, so I was satisfied! I grinned from ear to ear and said, "YES!"

Ms. Lois gave me her phone number and said that I could call anytime. I held onto it like it was gold. I didn't waste any time calling her. I had to sneak and do it, but I called her as soon as I got home. I started calling her every day when she got home from work. It never felt like she didn't want to talk to me. I didn't say much, but when I did she listened. I felt she really cared. She always told me she loved me, and it melted my heart every time. Although I was a teenager, I NEVER had anyone to tell me they loved me, so when she told me it was so soothing. I started calling her Mama Lois. It just felt right. I always made the phone calls from my parents' rooms. If I saw Deddy pulling up the driveway, I ended the call.

One particular day, I missed seeing him pulling up. "Who are you talking to?" Deddy sternly asked.

"I'm talking to my godmother."

"Who?" he asked confusingly.

Deddy was sho'nuff thrown for a loop when I told him who she was. He knew her, but he didn't know how or when this came about. He had so many questions, but I was panic-stricken with the next question.

"Do you remember what I told you? I will hurt you or anyone else you get involved."

I had gotten comfortable with Mama Lois and I do believe I might have told her had he not threatened me again. I loved this woman, and I truly didn't want the one person I felt cared about me to get hurt. Deddy only allowed me to call her on occasions, but what he didn't know was, I continued calling Mama Lois almost every day before he arrived home from work.

Deddy did his darndest to make sure that things looked as normal as possible to the outside world. He portrayed himself as a God-fearing man who was raising a God-fearing family. I remember having to listen to one of his sermons of him criticizing men for sexually abusing their kids. I wondered why God didn't strike him down at that very moment. If Deddy had completely cut Mama Lois off from me, that would have been a red flag. When I told Mama Lois that Deddy wouldn't let me call her every day, she started giving me stamps so I could write to her. I never told her *the secret* because I was just too afraid and did not want her to get hurt. I did give her clues about the abuse and hoped that she was going to be able to put two and two together.

One time I ran out of stamps and asked Deddy if he would buy one and take the letter to the post office. That was my only way to be able to get it to her. I didn't think I had anything to worry about since the letter was sealed.

"Okay," he answered anxiously. Mama Lois never received that letter and I know it wasn't because it got lost in the mail. Evidently, it wasn't much in the letter to make Deddy too suspicious. Look at God!

Mama Lois sincerely loved me. She gave me hugs, disciplined me when I needed it and showered me with much love. I got to spend nights at her house on occasions, and I was even able to take a trip with her that was two hours away! I know it worried Deddy that Mama Lois loved me the way she did, but once again, he had to make everything look normal.

When I moved from my parents' house, I finally shared the abuse with Mama Lois. She said she had suspected this might have gone on. Mama Lois said that she had even asked her husband, "Do you think the Rev is messing around with Sharon?"

"Naw, not the Rev!" her husband replied.

Deddy's "preacher" image was totally opposite of his "home" image, and he had the ability to deceive many. I am very confident that if Mama Lois had concrete evidence about the abuse, she would have come to my rescue. I used to blame myself for not telling her but realized I was just a scared and confused victim who wanted to protect her. I did not keep in touch with Mama Lois when I first left my parents' house. It was because I was dealing with a lot of confusion and was trying to find myself. About a year later, I reached back out to her and it was like we didn't miss a beat. She still loved and treated me like I was her very own.

I thought I was ready for some counseling, so I asked Mama Lois if she would come with me. Being the good person that she is she said yes. I had every intention of opening up and telling my story, but when I got there and saw that it was a man who was going to counsel me I froze. I froze, not because I was afraid to tell my story, but because it was a man. I was very uncomfortable with men. I did not trust men! I literally could not speak. It's like I was zapped back to that place Deddy used to take me. Mama Lois was quite disappointed that I didn't participate in the session. I totally understand why she was disappointed. We had to drive in two hours of heavy traffic and that didn't make it any better. I couldn't explain to her what was going on. It wasn't anything the counselor did. It wasn't even his fault that I felt that way. It's just that his presence gave me flashbacks. Later, when I got out of that funk, I was able to explain to Mama Lois what went on. I'm glad she was able to understand.

Mama Lois had seen Deddy at church one Sunday after my move. She asked him, "How is Sharon doing?"

Hoping to change her view of me, Deddy responded with, "Ah, you know Sharon is a lesbian now. She moved in with her lesbian friend."

Mama Lois was hot. "I don't believe it! I don't know what's going on but I'm going to find out!" she said.

Deddy was unable to convince Mama Lois, so he disappointedly walked away. Deddy had used the gay card on other occasions. He told me a few times, "If you don't give it to me my sickness is going to make me gay."

OMG! I cannot believe I believed him! It was unbelievable! He literally could make me believe just about anything he said. He also told me, "You don't need to be hanging with Lois. Do you see how she is always hugging and kissing on you? She must be gay."

Excuse me, that was solely pure love and affection! Deddy usually easily persuaded me, but I loved those hugs and kisses and didn't have any intentions of giving them up.

I keep in touch with Mama Lois now, but I must admit, I don't keep in touch like I should. There is one thing for sure though, Mama Lois will FOREVER be in my heart. I have told her many times I love her and always will no matter what. I also told her I am very grateful that God put her in my life, especially at the time that He did. He knew what He was doing. I love you, Mama Lois. Forever.

Although I was a genuine fighter, I found myself confused at times. Not at all times, but a few times. Sometimes I found myself having pleasure in the way my body responded. I couldn't understand why I felt excited about something I did not want. When Deddy finished his sin, I felt sad, guilty, and ashamed for the way my body responded. It wasn't until many years later during my healing process that I identified my body was merely reacting to the way God had the human body set up to react. Please know this. Just because my body responded does not mean it was consensual. It was very important for me to gain this in-depth interpretation to prepare me for my healing. I had to come to terms that it was not my fault that my body responded that way. I had to accept the fact that I was a victim and did absolutely nothing to deserve the abuse that had been inflicted upon me. I always fought with all my might, which I'm sure made things a lot worse for me. Deddy did not like that at all.

One day I fought so strenuously that my pants ripped and the zipper broke.

"Okay, I'll fix that," Deddy boasted.

I didn't know what he meant, but I found out later that night. Mama did not believe women should wear pants, but Janelle and I could wear them. Between the time Deddy ripped my pants and the time before I laid down for bed, he talked with Mama, telling her that he was on board with women not wearing pants.

A Bona Fide Conqueror

He also told her that he was putting a stop to Janelle and me wearing them. So, just like that, besides wearing shorts for gym class, we were not allowed to wear pants anymore. Deddy was sure to rub in my face what he had done. He *"fixed it"* by giving himself easier access to me.

Mama blissfully began to sew a collection of skirts and dresses for us to wear to school. Mama loved sewing, but she was not a first-class seamstress, bless her heart. What little pizzazz we did have took a prompt downward slope. Why? Why? Why? It was extremely cold on this one school morning.

"Deddy, it's so cold outside. Can we please, please wear pants today?" I pleaded.

I guess we held onto our pants, hoping we could go back to the way it was. It was several months after we started this ploy, but Deddy still had that "I'm making you pay" attitude. With a smirk on his face he said, "Nope. Y'all will never wear pants again." Thankfully by my senior year, he somehow had a change of heart. I don't know why he changed his mind, but I am SO glad he did. I'm ALSO glad we held on to those pants!

A Bona Fide Conqueror

DADDY DADDY, PLEASE GO AWAY

by Sharon Ramsey (Quarles)

Daddy Daddy, please don't touch me there
This is not something I am willing to share
You will share it, do you hear what I say
And if you tell, you will surely pay
But Daddy when you touch me it makes me cry
And when others are around I feel very shy
It's not that big of a deal
Go ahead reach down and get yourself a feel
I can't do that it's just not right
Please go away and let me have a peaceful night
Come here child and lay down
And don't let me hear you make one sound
Daddy, Daddy please go away
I'm tired of you touching me day after day
But you feel much better than your mother
Lay down I'm getting it one way or the other
We are blood kin don't you see
This is not the way it supposed to be
Don't you want to help me child
Relax, it will be over after a while
You act like you don't even care
What you are doing to me just isn't fair
See it's all over and it didn't take long
But don't you tell that will be so so wrong
I'm so confused I just have to pray
Daddy, Daddy please go away.

Chapter 4
I Got Away

Matthew 11:28 New Living Translation
Then Jesus said, "Come to me all of you who are weary and carry heavy burdens, and I will give you rest."

By now, I have graduated from high school. As it happened, I graduated on my eighteenth birthday in 1986.

"Can we eat at Long John Silver's for my graduation?" I asked Mama and Deddy in hopes of them saying 'Yes.'

They agreed, so I was very excited. I was going to Long John Silver's! I had never eaten at this restaurant; I just always heard people talk about it. We went to Long John Silver's right after graduation. The food smelled so delightful. I couldn't wait to dig in. I ordered my food and stepped aside to let everyone else order.

"Are you gonna pay?" Deddy imposed on me. At first, I thought this was a joke, but I not only had to pay for my meal, I had to pay for my entire family's meals. This was an insult. I sat at the table with low spirits. I thought I was going to be pampered for this memorable moment in my life. How cruel was it to make me pay for the meals just because I suggested.

A Bona Fide Conqueror

They were supposed to celebrate me, but I did not receive one gift for my birthday, let alone my graduation. On top of that, I was raped that night.

When Burger King first came to our little hometown in 1985, Deddy let me get a job there. It was one of the few restaurants in our town. Shannon also got a job at Burger King. I remained friends with her, but I quickly became friends with Christina. She was the night shift manager. Christina had such a bubbly personality, and she was very easy to get along with. She was not even supposed to be the manager in my town, but God had a plan.

As time passed, other than the secret, I began sharing with Christina things that went on in my household. My family was very dysfunctional, so I had plenty to share with her. I felt at ease talking with her about anything. Shannon was my very first friend. I withheld telling her about the abuse because of the threats Deddy made. I didn't tell her about my family drama because I didn't want to scare her away. Christina was five years older than Shannon and me. It most likely was the age difference that made it easier to talk to her. I looked up to her, regarding her with high esteem.

Before clocking out every night, the employees had to clean, break down equipment and stock up for the day shift. I was part of the management team, and it was my duty to make sure everyone was getting things done. When everyone clocked out and left the premises, there was just Christina and me in the building. I had my driver's license, which was a traumatizing experience by the way, and I drove to work. However, Deddy came and sat in the parking lot at least an hour before the shift ended and followed me home. He told Mama that I was being "fass," hot in the pants, if you will, so he needed to keep an eye on me. *The lies!!!* It was only that one guy, and he didn't know about him. He just made sure I didn't have sex with guys because he thought he "owned" me. Remember, Christina didn't know *the secret,* so in her mind she thought maybe I was a wild child. I later found out she had a hard time accepting that because of my good work ethics. I stayed in the office with Christina until she finished all her paperwork. I don't know what all she had to do, but it usually took her up to two hours to finish. She was a perfectionist.

Since I was a part of management, it was easy to convince Deddy that I had paperwork I had to complete before leaving. Because I was sleep-deprived, when I was in the office I bunched up in a ball on the floor and fell asleep. I slept until Christina finished up all her paperwork. As a result of feeling safe and secure, that was some of the best sleep. It always saddened me when she woke me up to leave. I had to suck it up because I couldn't let Deddy see the sadness on my face.

I loved being on night shift, but when Christina switched to the day shift, I followed right behind her. I had grown very fond of her. One day she didn't have to work, but I really needed to see her. I called her to ask if I could come see her. Christina gave me her address and I told her I was coming right after work. I tensely made a call to Deddy and told him that I had to work over. I didn't waste any time clocking out. I got in my car and headed straight to Christina's apartment. When I arrived, I didn't stay long because I knew I was taking a big risk. Christina lived in a different city, so I also had to take that into consideration. Whew! I made it home! I thought I had made it back without any problems, but boy was I wrong! Deddy stepped from the front porch and came over to the car.

He stuck his head inside the car and then asked me, "Where you been?"

I started having heart palpitations. "Uhohhh." I thought. Had Deddy gone to my job and seen that my car wasn't there?

I didn't know but I responded with, "I told you I had to work over."

He then said in a demeaning manner, "I know what you said, but I checked the odometer before you left for work. It doesn't take that many miles for you to get to work."

So that's what he was looking at. This man had been checking my mileage before I left for work. Wow, who does that? I took a deep breath. How was I going to get out of this? I had to think quickly on my toes, but I had no clue that my next response was going to be an epic failure.

"I had to back up because a car was in my way."

I knew what I had done, and I knew that putting my car in reverse would not have put all those miles on the odometer. But listen, that's all I had.

"Distance isn't calculated when the car is in reverse, so I'm gonna ask you again. Where have you been?" Deddy sternly asked.

I had no choice but to tell him where I had been. I ended up disclosing my whereabouts to him, but to my surprise he just said, "You gonna have to pay for this tonight."

Of course, that meant paying for it through another rape. The strategy was to make me feel like I brought it on myself.

I increasingly had the desire to share *the secret* with Christina. The threat Deddy had made to me about hurting me or anyone else I told constantly ran through my mind. However, there was something that kept compelling me to tell her. That something was undoubtedly the Holy Spirit. The Holy Spirit was helping me even when I didn't see it. I waited until I knew without a shadow of a doubt that I could trust her with *the secret*.

"Christina, I need to talk to you about something really, really important," I nervously said to her.

"Okay," she said. "I'll be here. Let me know when you want to talk."

When I had a moment, I walked to Christina's office prepared to tell her *the secret*.

"Are you ready to tell me what you wanted to tell me?" Christina asked.

When I opened my mouth, absolutely nothing came out.

"I can't do it; I'm scared. I'll tell you later."

I was extremely nervous. Every time I went to talk to her, I froze up and walked away and said, "I'm scared. I'll tell you later."

Christina had become very frustrated because I

would never tell her. I was desperate to tell her, especially since she was leaving the state in a couple days. I didn't tell her that day, but I had the idea to write her a letter. I wrote the letter and put it on the side of her pocketbook. I called her later that night.

Ring Ring.

"Hello," Christina answered. "Did you read your letter?"

Confused, Christina asked, "What letter?"

"I wrote you a letter to tell you what I wanted you to know. I dropped it on the side of your pocketbook."

"Okay, I'll go read it now," she said.

I waited anxiously to get her feedback. I was still extremely nervous. I didn't know what the after-effects would be. I didn't want Christina to get hurt. I was hoping I did the right thing. Christina read the letter and when I sneaked to call her later that night, she told me that if Deddy touched me again I needed to say I was going to tell. This may not have been the best advice because she wasn't trained for this type of situation. Since Christina was leaving the state momentarily, she didn't have a clue as to what to do. She wanted to protect me, but she was leaving. She brought me to the office and then she called the Department of Social Services. They told her that because of my age they couldn't do anything. They said the only thing they could recommend is for me to press charges against Deddy and that I needed to get out right then. I was afraid to press charges because of the threats Deddy had made, so I didn't. Without knowing it, right before Christina left, she

A Bona Fide Conqueror

made a tactical choice to tell Jimmy, the store manager, the situation so that he could monitor the situation. Sharing *the secret* with Christina gave me willpower. I was determined to get out of this situation. It was as if she had sown a seed in me that produced courage. The abuse continued, but I didn't quite have the courage to say I was going to tell. I gave a more hostile fight, however.

When Christina returned from her trip three days later, I had the chance to share with her details about the abuse. She encouraged me to break free from the abuse. I wanted to, but where was I to go? It made sense to her now why Deddy always came to wait for me before I got off. Christina didn't think I was a bad, wild child. She told me once more to tell Deddy I was going to tell if he touched me again. I was ready this time. Enough was enough!

It was on a cold, February evening when Deddy and I were in the house alone. He came into my room.

"What are you doing?" He asked.

I could tell in his voice that he was ready to do his dirt, but I was ready for him. Had I known we were going to be in the house alone, I would have left with Mama. That was the thing; Deddy had a way of getting us in the house alone without me even knowing it. He started touching me, and I felt the fear begin to creep up in me. To say I was going to tell didn't come out as easily as I thought it would. As I continued to feel his touches, anger began to set in. I had to convince myself this was going to be the last time. I kept hearing Christina's voice saying, "If he touches you again, say you're going to tell."

The boldness began to stir up and before I knew it, I used my legs to give him a striking push as I screamed out, "I'M GOING TO TELL!"

To my surprise, Deddy just left my room. I will never forget the thought I had at that moment. Wow, if I knew it would be this easy, I would have done this a long time ago! I remained seated on my bed feeling both a sense of relief and a sense of pride. I did it! I thought. I don't have to worry about Deddy messing with me again!

Within a few minutes, those feelings quickly changed to anxiety. Deddy came back into my room looking a little deranged, and he was holding a gun. He put the gun to my head and asked, "You gonna do what?"

My heart felt as though it were pounding out of my chest, while the rest of my body felt paralyzed. I tried to shout out, "I WON'T TELL!" But I was too dumbfounded to utter those words. Deddy withdrew the gun from my head and aggressively plunged it into my hand, clenching my scrawny finger on the trigger. As my finger rested reluctantly on the trigger, I was careful not to make one move, terrified the gun might go off. Then, in a sober voice Deddy said, "No, you can just kill me." Lastly, he placed the gun to his head and declared, "I'll kill myself."

My childlike mind desperately tried to absorb everything that had transpired right before me. As things were happening, I marvelled at the fact that I might die for boldly blurting out, I was going to tell. I wondered, "Is he really about to fulfill his promise?"

I was even more disturbed when he flipped the

script, trying to coerce me to kill him and then ultimately suggesting that he would kill himself. Was he wanting me to feel the guilt and live with that memory for the rest of my life? Whatever Deddy's plan was, I was damned regardless. Instantaneously, I gained a morsel of hope when I saw Mama driving up the driveway. Despite me never having the dependability of Mama being there for me when I needed her, I desperately tried to keep that newfound hope alive in that moment.

When Deddy saw me looking out the window he took a glance to see what I was looking at. As he was speedily leaving the room, he forewarned me, "You better not say a word!"

The very moment Deddy was out of my sight, I broke out in an uncontrollable cry. He rushed back to my room shortly before Mama entered the house. He frantically began to pace the floor.

"Shut up! Shut up! You better not get me in trouble!" he murmured.

At this point, there was nothing he could do or say to restrain me from crying. This was a cry of anguish and despair that wasn't going to be easily suppressed. My eyes were blurred with tears, but I caught a glimpse of Mama and Janelle standing in the doorway. I thought maybe, just maybe this was the time to reveal to Mama all the hell I've been enduring from this man for nearly six years. In a dull and passionless voice Mama asked me, "Girl, what's wrong with you?"

I desperately wanted to tell her. I wanted to tell her everything, but much to my inclination, the only thing that came out of my mouth because of fear was,

"Nothing."

What if Deddy's plan was to kill me if I told? Heck, what if his plan was to kill Mama, Janelle and me if I opened my mouth to let out *the secret*? Yes, Mama and my relationship was debilitated, but I was hoping that Mama would finally rescue me. Instead, after she heard me say nothing was wrong, she just closed the door and walked away. That newfound hope I had gained followed right out the door with her. It truly broke my heart. I mean, I was immune to not having love from her, but the moment she shut the door took me to a brand new low. She was automatically supposed to protect me. I was automatically supposed to have her trust her to protect me. I did not die that day, but I was afraid that day could come soon.

"Sharon, what's wrong? Tell me what's wrong!" Janelle pleaded with me.

I could see the genuine concern Janelle displayed, but the wedge Deddy put between us was so deep that I did not trust it. I kept *the secret*.

The next morning, I told the only person who I had told *the secret* to what went on the night before.

"Sharon, this has gotten too dangerous!"

Christina called the DSS office again to let them know about the gun situation. They told me to get out fast and go live with a trusted source. I had nobody! I had nowhere to go. DSS staff said don't go back to the house to try to get anything, but if I must go back, to go when I knew Deddy wasn't home.

"Sharon, you can come stay with me."

Now look how God works! Christina's roommate had just moved out, so she had an empty bedroom to spare. I was terrified, but I knew this was my way out. The very next morning, I made my move.

When the car was warming up from the cold, I had to press the gas from time to time so it wouldn't cut off. This morning, I went out at least four times. I pressed the gas, but I also put the clothes I had stuffed inside my coat inside the car. These were the clothes I was taking with me. I was so afraid of getting caught. I was jittery the whole day at work.

After work, I left my car in the parking lot and rode with Christina to get settled in to my soon-to-be-residence. I was a nervous wreck. I waited until later that night before I called to tell Mama and Deddy I wasn't coming home.

Ring Ring.

"Hello," Mama answered.

"Mama, I'm not coming home."

"Girl, you better get yourself home. Your daddy been out there looking for you all day."

Having Mama to tell me that Deddy had been looking for me made me that much more anxious. Was he searching for me to hurt me like he'd always promised? I don't know, but I knew at that point I was not going back. Mama continued pestering me, telling me to come home.

"Mama, I'm serious. I'm not coming back home!" I informed her.

I heard Janelle in the background saying, "What is it? What's wrong?"

Mama began to answer her, "Sharon said she wasn't coming home, I told her..." but Janelle quickly grabbed the phone.

"Sharon, what is it? Why aren't you coming home?"

I never answered, but kept repeating to Janelle, "I'm just not coming back!"

As I continued hearing Mama saying in the background that I better come home, I grew more and more fed up and agitated. I finally blurted out to Janelle, "I'm not coming home because Deddy has been messing with me!!!"

CLUNK!! Janelle flung the phone to the floor. "NOOOOO!!!!" Janelle screamed.

Janelle got back on the phone and said, "Deddy been messing with me, too! He told me that he wasn't messing with you!"

"Well, he told me that he wasn't messing with you!" I said mystifyingly. My intuition was finally confirmed. Deddy had been messing with my sister!

"Sharon do not come home. Stay where you are," Janelle exclaimed.

"Call me back later," she said and then she hung up the phone.

Deddy plainly told me he wasn't messing with Janelle and told Janelle he wasn't messing with me. Deddy started fondling Janelle when she was nine, but started penetrating her when she was thirteen, a year before he started penetrating me. I strongly believe that Deddy used to fondle me before the age of thirteen. I used to have these vivid images in my head of me sitting on his lap, him tickling me and of him giving me long hugs. The whole scene never played out completely in my head, but it would appear as if I was always uncomfortable. Once again, I was told I had suppressed memories and I believe this was one of them.

More or less than a decade ago, I cross-examined Deddy. I told him about the half memories and asked him if he had ever touched me inappropriately before the age of thirteen. He answered, "No," but the peculiar look on his face and all the jabber that came along with his answer convinced me that I was not just imagining things. Janelle had the same hunch that Deddy was messing with me as I had of him messing with her. But just as he had me brain-washed, he had Janelle brain-washed as well. One reason he always bought her gifts was to put that wedge between us. He did not want us to talk about what was going on. He knew that if we got together, we would be a force to be reckoned with. Buying those gifts was also Deddy's way of luring Janelle into his scheme. He bought her gifts to receive sexual favors. Janelle told me that she used to always pray that this was not happening to me. She wanted to protect me. I felt badly that I was on the verge of hating her. It perturbed me to know that Deddy had me feeling that way towards my sister all because he wanted to do his evil. How sick is that?

"Come on, Mama," Janelle demanded.

"Where are we going?" asked curious Mom.

"Mama, just get in the car!"

Janelle and Mama got in the car and headed to the police station. Janelle didn't tell Mama where they were headed. She figured that Mama more than likely would have refused to come along if she knew where she was going. When they arrived at the police station,

A Bona Fide Conqueror

Mama asked, "Why are we here?"

Janelle continued walking into the station without answering, and then she headed to the window. Janelle didn't know what to do, but she walked up to one of the officers and said, "I want to report that Deddy been messing with me and my sister."

When Mama heard that she went into a full-blown panic. "Janelle, don't do this! How will this look on your daddy?"

Sad. Mama was not concerned about her hurting daughters, but she was very much concerned about the man who hurt her daughters. She kept pleading with Janelle to drop the charges. This was very raw. Janelle was fragile and didn't yet have a backbone. Because of that, Mama was able to persuade her to drop the charges. The chief officer was pissed at Mama. He was pissed because he knew Deddy. In all likelihood, he did not know that the abuse was going on, but now that he did he wanted Deddy to pay.

When it was uncovered what Deddy had done to me, I had people disrespectfully ask me, "Why did you put up with the abuse for so long?" or "Why didn't you tell anyone?"

Yes, I was eighteen, but eighteen with the mind of a child. I most definitely wanted out, but I felt trapped. I was brain-washed by Deddy. He had complete control over my mind. My body. He controlled my behavior. Deddy groomed me into the person he wanted me to be. It was almost like I was a robot. He controlled my whole being. Period.

When I called Janelle later that night, she said that Deddy was still out looking for me. She let me know what took place at the police station. I was infuriated knowing that Mama would rather protect her husband who hurt her daughters instead of protecting her daughters who got hurt by her husband. Janelle, Roy and Brandon informed me that Deddy was constantly pacing the floor and hitting the walls when he finally returned home. He was nervous thinking that everything was about to come crashing down.

When I returned to work the next day, Mama came to talk to me, still begging me to come back home. Christina took Mama to her office to talk to her. Christina told Mama that I did not need to be in that dangerous situation.

"God will take care of this," Mama told Christina.

"God already has taken care of it by getting Sharon out of the bad situation!" Christina pleaded.

At some point, Janelle said that Deddy claimed that the devil had put in his mind to kill everybody and then kill himself. I guess Deddy was feeling out of harm's way because he came to my job and begged me to come home. He said what he did in the very beginning, "I promise, it won't happen again."

If it happened practically every day for almost six years, what made him think I would believe him now? The boldness remained in me so in a serious and stern voice I said, "I am never coming back home!" I thought my message had been received by him loud and clear.

He then said, "If you change your mind, you can come home anytime you want."

He began to walk out the door, but turned back around and said, "You didn't have to leave the car.

It's yours." Then he proceeded to walk out the door.

I was relieved to see him go. Oh, and I did take the car. I thought he had received my message loud and clear, but a few months later when I went to visit Mama something happened. I pulled up. I saw Mama's car in the yard and Deddy's truck was gone. When I stepped inside the house, I got a surprise. Deddy was sitting in his brown recliner with his legs propped up. Deddy never let Mama drive his truck, but for whatever reason she had driven it that day. I immediately stopped in my tracks.

"Where's Mama," I asked.

"Ah, I let her drive my truck to the shopping center."

"Alright. I'll see you later."

"Wait a minute!" Deddy exclaimed.

"My back been giving me some trouble and I was wondering…"

I began to get nervous, but I bellowed out, "I'm not rubbing your back! Bye!"

I quickly rushed out the door and was in my car before he was able to stand up to look out the door. I could not believe he had the audacity to try to reel me back into his sick, little game. I knew right then that this man was never to be trusted. I continued going to visit Mama because I still desired to find that connection with her. But when I went, I kept my distance from Deddy. Was this the way it was going to be for the rest of my life?

A Bona Fide Conqueror

EVERYBODY NEEDS SOMEONE

by Sharon Ramsey (Quarles)

Everybody needs someone
Someone to talk with someone to hug
Mainly someone to love
When you are feeling depressed
And you find there's no need for rest
That's the time you call
That special someone
And tell it all
If you feel you can't talk
Just write them a letter
I'm sure either way will make you feel better
If you don't have a special someone but you feel
alone
Please go out and find them
Before you find yourself gone

Chapter 5
Life After the Abuse

John 10:10 New Living Translation
The thief's purpose is to steal and kill and destroy. My purpose is to give life in all its fullness.

Janelle left less than a week after I moved out to get herself out of the situation. We were free! Free! Free! Or so I thought. It was a major adjustment trying to figure out how life was really supposed to be lived. It was appearing to be in a continuous downward spiral. The aftermath of abuse had me headed for self-destruction. I became very promiscuous. I was having sex with guys because I was searching for L-O-V-E. I usually didn't find sexual pleasure from the acts. It was just that, an act. I felt obligated to please the guys. I wonder what made me feel that way. Mmhmm. Plus, I thought that if I pleased them, somehow they might want to stay with me. Well, that never happened. Other times, I was too afraid to tell them, "No." I had in my head that they would get it whether I chose to give it to them or not. That happened a few times. When I chose not to give it to them, I literally got raped.

This made me think about another incident I had

with one of my cousins. I saw my cousin walking down the road, so I pulled over to ask him if he needed a ride to where he was going. He took my offer and happened in the car. We were having a casual conversation, catching up because we had not seen each other for a while.

"Girl, you sure are looking good. You grew up on me," he said.

He reached over and put his hand in my panties. I was automatically taken to that place. Yes, I had been having promiscuous affairs, but I believe because this was a family member it took me to that place. My car had almost come to a complete stop because I froze. Somehow, I was able to snap back.

"Get out of my car!" I cold-bloodily demanded him. I was furious, but I was proud at the same time for having the willpower to do that. I kept driving, feeling very frustrated.

Will it ever end? I asked myself. I did not know how to live. I was a big follower. I didn't know how to fit in. Shoot, I didn't fit in. I didn't really have friends, but the people I interacted with, I did things to please them no matter how it made me look or feel. I agreed with everything they said, even if I knew it was wrong. I did this because I was afraid of not being accepted.

The things I was experiencing back then were a ripple effect from what I experienced earlier in life. I thank my Heavenly Father for allowing me not to sink into dire temptations.

Still working at Burger King, I continued living with Christina. Christina and I had no issues living together. We got along great. Company frequented the apartment. I wasn't used to that. Christina loved to party. I wasn't used to that, but I soon became accustomed to it and fit right in. The issue I had when I drank was I ended up crying for some reason. But other than that, I was a tolerable drunk.

"I hit a dog y'all!" I candidly confessed.

A group of us were gathered at the apartment, as usual, drinking and having fun. I shared that I had hit a dog because I was wanting some sympathy. I was sad I had hit and possibly killed that poor dog. My conscience wanted me to fess up.

"Curiosity killed the cat and Sharon killed the dog!" Golden jokingly said out loud.

Why did he say that? I jumped up and ran my tipsy behind right out the door. I was running down the road crying as Susan and Jordan chased me.

"Come back! Come back!" they yelled.

Susan was one of my work buddies who I had grown close to. She and her cousin, Jordan, continued chasing me until they were able to catch me. They comforted me and led me back to the apartment. We were able to laugh about it later, but they knew I was a sensitive drunk.

I had much respect for Christina, and I never had plans to hurt her. I felt indebted to her. Christina allowing me to move in with her to escape my abuse was truly a blessing I will forever be grateful for. Susan stayed with me at the apartment while we were waiting for Christina to get home from work. Pretty soon, the guy Christina talked to and one of his buddies stopped by. Christina's guy took me to her room while Susan was stuck somewhere with the other guy. It was almost like it was a set up. Susan refused to go along with what was presented, but it didn't take much to reel me in. I did not have sexual intercourse with the guy, but something happened that made me regret it and feel I violated Christina's trust. In a short time, Christina came home and caught us in her bedroom.

"What's going on?" Christina demanded.

We responded at the same time, "Nothing."

Christina knew something wasn't adding up, but she let it go for the moment. I felt so horrible for what I had done. Why didn't I tell that guy, "No?" Oh yeah, I didn't know how to say, "No." I was scared to say, "No." As God be my witness, I did not mean to betray the one person that got me out of the worst situation of my life.

Christina soon found out what happened. It was explained to her that I was the pursuer. I admit what went on wasn't right. I wasn't forced; however the act was done because I frankly didn't know how to reject his invitation.

Christina was quite upset with me and I understood. I know she felt betrayed. I know she was hurt because the person she helped caused her pain. I really wanted her to understand I didn't do it deliberately. It was done out of mental weakness.

That night, when everyone came over for the usual event, Christina chose to ridicule me in front of the crowd. I thought I was handling it fairly well, but I absolutely lost it when she said, "You're a whore. You probably liked what your daddy did to you."

I was very humiliated and ashamed. First, I couldn't believe she basically let the whole group know what my daddy had done to me. Secondly, I couldn't believe she said I enjoyed it after everything I had shared with her. I confided in Christina and that crushed me. Now, I felt betrayed. I was devastated. I'm not making excuses for Christina, but although she was older, we were both still young. Her actions stemmed from wanting to get even with me. Likewise, I am not making excuses for myself, but my actions were due to lack of knowledge.

The abuse in my life caused me to make that terrible mistake with Christina's friend. I can relate to this now, but back then, the humiliation that came from Christina caused me to grab my pocketbook, storm into my car and speed off without looking back. Now that I'm reminiscing, I just realized no one came after me. Just because people party with you does not mean they are your friends. Those words Christina said kept replaying in my head the whole drive. I indeed wanted to die. I drove down the dark, deserted highway contemplating how I wanted to die.

"I hate my life!" I kept telling myself. I almost made the conscious decision to run my car in the lake, but for some odd reason I decided to think about my life a little more, so I continued driving.

When I arrived at what appeared to be a safe location on the dark and dreary road, my car suddenly began to smoke heavily and stalled immediately. It was around four o'clock in the morning. I was afraid because I'd never been out at that time alone. If I could only make it to the grocery store, I murmured to myself. The grocery store was about a fourth of a mile down the road. I wanted to try to make it there to make a phone call. This was way before cell phones. I didn't know who I was going to call, but I just needed to get there. I started walking, but I was being very vigilant.

When I looked back and saw a car slowly creeping up to me, I began to run. I fell like the women in the movies. The struggle of trying to stay on my feet was real. I fell, got back up again, then fell again. The guy stopped his car right beside me.

"Do you need some help?" he politely asked.

"No, I'm okay."

"Is that your car back there?"

"Yes, it is. I'm going to the store to call someone right now."

"Ma'am, I can see that you need help. Let me help you. It's too dangerous for you to be out here. I promise I will take you wherever you need to go."

God really does have a way of doing things that are mighty sweet. Just think, minutes prior I was ready to end my life. But now, I was afraid of possibly losing my life. God put me in that situation to let me know I was not ready to die. I just needed to calm down.

At the same time, He sent me help because it wasn't His plan for me to die. If I would have continued the drive, I would've had more time to think of all the misfortunes in my life. I would've taken my life ahead of God's appointed time. I finally accepted the guy's assistance. I got in the car so he could take me where I needed to go. The thing is, I didn't know where to go, but it hit me. I can go to

Shannon's house. I told him the way to go. Shannon was like two miles up the road from where we were.

At that time, I didn't look at the guy as being an angel God had sent, even when he told me he wasn't usually out at that time of morning. I kept my hand on the door handle in case I needed to jump out of the car. I prayed that if I did jump out, it wouldn't be like in the movies. You know, where the door won't open. I made it safely to Shannon's and stayed there for the rest of the morning.

Christina and I did restore our friendship, but we never really resolved or talked about the issue. We left it covered for many, many years. When I started writing this chapter, I didn't realize the hurt was still consuming me. I was led by the Holy Spirit to give her a call. I had a chance to further explain to her what I was going through at that time, and I also had a chance to apologize to her again. In return, Christina also apologized to me. I'm writing this book to help others, but God has been using this book to help me get rid of baggage that I didn't even know I had. I can truly say that Christina and I both had a chance to release. I love you, Christina!!

I only lived with Christina for a few months. She was the angel God sent to get me out of the bad situation, but it was time for me to move on. When I told Janelle what happened between Christina and me, she let me move in with her. Janelle was staying in an apartment. She had recently gotten engaged, and this is where she and her soon-to-be husband were going to live. Janelle was being the "real" big sister she always wanted to be. She wanted to rescue me, and that is just what she did.

I continued working at Burger King after the fallout with Christina. She had to talk to me since she was my boss. We eventually made up, but it just wasn't the same.

"Sharon, come here when you get a chance, please," Jimmy told me.

"Wow! I hope I'm not in trouble," I thought to myself.

As soon as my work was caught up, I worriedly walked over to the table where Jimmy was sitting to see what he wanted.

"Go ahead, have a seat," he said. I followed his direction and took a seat. "Don't be upset, but Christina told me about your dad. I am here for you."

I couldn't believe Christina told Jimmy about Deddy. I can understand her reasoning now, but when I found out back then it made me feel betrayed. I appreciate her trying to protect me, although Jimmy ended up using it to his advantage.

"She told me to see if I could help you. I think you are a beautiful person and I have become attracted to you," he said maliciously.

I couldn't see it then, but I now realize I was victimized. He had been scoping me out since the time Christina told him about Deddy. Jimmy knew that I was weak. He knew I didn't have that fatherly love that every young girl needs. He knew it would be easy for him to get my attention. Jimmy said he wanted to help. In my eyes, Jimmy was being no better than my daddy. But guess what? I walked right into his trap. I was this skinny, black, young girl and he was this skinny, white, *older* guy. Oh yeah, he was married. Why would he be attracted to me? I didn't know, but I liked the feeling it gave me.

After work, I met Jimmy at a familiar spot and then he led me to a secluded field. We talked a while and then we kissed. Sex was not involved that day, but the next time we met it was. I was spun into his web. I think Jimmy wanted it to be a one-time affair, but it lasted for nearly a year. Did I feel bad because I was having sex with a married man? Yes. Did I want it to stop? Yes and no. Jimmy started making me feel so special. He knew what to say and when to say it. Sounds familiar? Jimmy's wife had already known about my situation because they tried to help me. I had already gone to their house for visits. I really felt bad, but the infatuation I had for Jimmy made me want to continue the affair.

Then, the unexpected happened. I became pregnant. As much as I knew this was wrong, I was super excited to be having his baby. He told me that he would pay if I wanted to terminate the pregnancy. I had no plans of doing that. I was about to have something I could call my own and that gave me happiness. Well, things changed a few weeks later. I had a miscarriage. God knew that the baby would have caused me a lot more pain. I didn't look at it that way then. I was upset and that gave me more reason to be mad at God.

I talked to Jimmy's wife on a regular basis. She had become my confidant. It may sound unorthodox, but it was true. I shared with her a lot of what I had gone through and what I was feeling. I let her know how upset I was with my parents and God. I let her know I often thought of suicide. I confided in her a lot, but I was sleeping with her husband. Father God, thank You for your forgiveness and Your protection. I made a call to her one day.

Ring Ring.

"Hello," she answered.

"Hello. I was wondering if it would be alright if I stopped by?" I asked.

"I found your work visor in Jimmy's car. Is there anything you need to tell me?"

Boy, I wasn't expecting this. I had to come up with something quick. "Umm, he had to take me home the other day and I must've left it on accident."

"Okay, but if I find out something is going on between y'all, you won't have to worry about killing yourself. I'll do it for you!" she said expressively.

I became very frantic when I heard those words. I had never had anything said to me like that. Although I was frightened, I continued the affair. She told Jimmy that one of us had to leave Burger King, so I decided I would be the one to leave.

I was raised in church, so I knew right from wrong. I knew what I was doing was wrong. I felt I couldn't live without Jimmy. The devil used this affair to help me cope with the pain. I thought I was running to what I thought was "love." The devil fed that powerful lie to me and I was relaxed in it. He also fed me other lies: "Why do you want to please God when he wasn't there for you?" "You never had love. This is how love feels." "Jimmy is helping you cope with the pain." "It can be y'alls secret. She won't find out."

A Bona Fide Conqueror

  I listened to the devil. I wanted to satisfy my flesh. I wasn't worried about the outcome, so I continued the affair in spite of the ultimatum. God saw that I did not heed the warning, so He got me out of it a few weeks later. Jimmy and I had made plans to meet. He always said he would leave a note if something came up and he couldn't make it. Well, when I didn't see him after a while, I checked where he said the note would be left, and to my surprise a note was there. It said that he was not coming, and he would not be able to see me anymore. I was devastated, but like always, my life continued. Like always, I am grateful that God was protecting me even when I didn't realize He was.

  When I quit working at Burger King, I began working at the plant where Mama and Deddy used to work. I was making a lot more money, so it was a good move for me. After a few months of working, I was able to get an apartment. I was finally able to accomplish something on my own. I was proud of myself, especially after hearing Deddy say I wouldn't be able to make it on my own. When the car Deddy gave me broke down on the side of the road months earlier, it was due to a blown motor. I didn't know I was supposed to put oil in the car, so…I purchased a used, white Ford Taurus. It wasn't the fanciest car, but it was a good car, and I was proud to call it my own. Things were starting to look up for me.

  After bragging to Carolyn, a friend from Burger King, how much I liked my new job, she soon joined the team. Guess what? We ended up being partners! Carolyn and I had become friends at Burger King, but after working at the plant we became inseparable.

A Bona Fide Conqueror

Usually if you saw her, you would see me and vice versa. Our shift was from three-thirty until eleven-thirty pm, and we would start our shenanigans right after we got off. It was a good shift if you liked to party, which we did. We always had something going on, whether it meant going to a club, hanging out at a late-night diner or hanging out at each other's residence. Most of the time, I had people over and we sat around, drank and played cards. This was during the week. Imagine what the weekend was like.

    My friend Shannon had started spending most of her time with her boyfriend during this time. I noticed that God always brought someone in my life so that I wouldn't be completely alone. When Shannon started dating and was slowly drifting away, He brought Christina. When Christina left, He brought Carolyn. He's a Good, Good Father! I was happy for Shannon, but I did miss her company. When I was able to spend time with her, I didn't get to experience doing normal "friendship" things with her. We basically just talked. Deddy didn't let us go anywhere except school, church and occasionally a walk around the neighborhood. Sometimes, we could go with Mama to the shopping center, but that was about it.

    Christina was a good person, and she is a good person until this day. I enjoyed every moment I spent with her, minus that one incident we had. But God's main reason for bringing her in my life was to rescue me and because of this, I didn't get to know her very well, either.

    Now Carolyn's friendship was totally different. She was in my life just for a season as well, but it was a longer and more productive season. I got to know her a lot better. Not that I didn't appreciate Shannon and Christina's friendships, but I gained a fresh new meaning of friendship with Carolyn. I had that authentic closeness with her, and it was unfamiliar to me. So, I was afraid of losing it.

While Carolyn never did or said anything to make me think I was going to lose her, I was just afraid. Deddy used to rule my life, but when I broke free of him, I still wasn't living my life freely. I was now imitating Carolyn's life. I was not comfortable in my own skin. Instead of executing my own happiness, I tried to be happy through her. Anything, she did I was sure to follow. Not only that, but I had also become very possessive of her. I tried not to let it be noticeable, but I can now look back and recognize that it was very noticeable! I didn't want to be that way and I tried to stop, but I couldn't. I finally had an authentic friend, and I did not want to lose her. Because of how I was wired, I couldn't comprehend that my actions could have easily caused her to want to leave. It had to be a God thing to keep her there. When Carolyn did things with me, I felt like I was wanted. When I saw her having fun with others, it felt like a threat. I always assumed she would throw me aside and forget about me. I didn't know anything about having a friend, so I didn't know anything about sharing. I was in blissful ignorance not knowing I was smothering Carolyn. I didn't want to share her, and I wanted all her attention. I was so desperate that one day, I negotiated a deal with her.

"If you move in with me, you don't have to pay

any bills."

I knew that it wouldn't have been a problem for her to split the bills with me. We worked together bringing home the same pay, so I knew how much she made. I was just that desperate to always have her in my presence. Carolyn did end up taking my offer, but in the long run she got married and moved to another state where her husband was enlisted.

The move was extremely hard for me. We basically did everything together. Carolyn knew the move was going to be hard for me, so she arranged for people to come check on me from time to time. Carolyn knew that I had been molested, but I never shared with her the whole story. We were more about the partying. The partying is what soothed my pain and when I wasn't partying, I had Carolyn as a backup. More releases have come to me during the time of writing this book. We had a chance to talk, and I had a chance to apologize to her for my behavior. She even apologized for some of hers. God is so God!

I continued pushing on through life, and I was amazed at how well I was doing without Carolyn. I began to make new friends, and they thought I was hilarious. My personality had started to form. I didn't even know I was that comical. I still had issues to work out, but I began to like myself a little. So, I was finding a little happiness. I wasn't partying anymore and was attempting to figure out life, and I made the decision to try out the third shift. I tried it and I loved it! Time moved on and I began to have a different outlook on life. Thank you, LORD, for giving me a new perspective on life.

Chapter 6
The Set Up

1 Corinthians 13:13 New Living Translation
There are three things that will endure- faith, hope, and love- and the greatest is love.

As time progressed, I continued to get myself together even more. I was between my early and mid-twenties and was just starting to learn how to live a basic life. I had challenging days for sure, but when I began to make even more new friends it gave me greater hope. I was very proud of myself for not being afraid to make new friends. It may seem minor, but that was a huge step for me. *Go, Sharon!*

I often visited Janelle. We tried to work on our toxic relationship. This one day when I went for a visit, a friend of Janelle's husband, Carl, was there.

When Erin left, Carl said to me, "Sharon, Erin wants to take you out."

"Ewww!" I spoke. "I don't want to go out with him!"

I had not dated that much, but he didn't seem to be my type. Now that I think about it, I sure was being picky to try to have "a type." I should've been thrilled that someone wanted to take me out. Oh well. Besides Jimmy and Tyler, no one had ever shown interest in me. Tyler was a guy that I had dated for less than a year, and he was four years younger than me. It's safe to say that he broke it off with me because he could not deal with my baggage. I'm telling you I was a solid mess.

When Carl told me that Erin wanted to take me out, it scared me. It scared me because I knew that guys usually only wanted one thing. I was getting to a place where I was learning to say "No" to them. It was my desire to stay away from all of that. It also scared me because I hadn't yet learned how to decode if someone had actual interest in me. Erin kept pestering Carl to persuade me to have a change of heart. I finally was suckered into giving him a try. I didn't like Erin in the beginning, but the more I went out with him the more I began to have feelings for him. We eventually became a couple. Just like Tyler, Erin had a hard time dealing with all my mood swings and everything else that came with the trauma of abuse.

Time passed and we began to have arguments, so his visits began to diminish. I wasn't feeling good about our relationship at this point, but I didn't expect what happened next.

Ring Ring.

"Hello," Erin answered.

"Hey. I took a pregnancy test and I'm pregnant."

Erin became very quiet over the phone. I discerned that he was in shock and that he was disappointed. He acted as if this was the worst thing I could have told him. I wanted the baby. I was still longing for something I could call my own. I thought that having a baby would give me the happiness I craved. I was distraught that Erin didn't feel excited about the baby.

Days later, I drove myself to the emergency room. I was in unbearable pain. I was praying that it was not another miscarriage. I waited patiently in the waiting room until finally, I was able to get a room. After I had already waited for an extended time, I had to wait even longer before I saw the doctor. I was curled up on the bed in a fetal position in intense pain. I heard the nurses talking, laughing and having a jolly good time. I was praying that one of them would come so they could check on me. The pain was very unbearable. I managed to look to see what it was I felt running down my leg. It was blood. I knew at that point my worst fear was happening. I was having a miscarriage. The pain continued and the nurses continued having a blast. I kept calling out, but because my voice was faint, they could not hear me. I managed to crawl to the door to obtain help.

"Please help me," I cried out in desperation.

The nurses looked at me like, "How dare you come out of that room." I didn't come out of the room. I was begging for help on the floor in the doorway. None of them scuttled to my rescue and offered to help me up off the floor.

"The doctor will be in there shortly," expressed one of the nurses.

"But it hurt so badly," I pleaded.

"I will page the doctor. Go back to the room."

At that point I felt irrelevant and disregarded, especially when no one offered to help me back into the room. I literally had to crawl back in the room and place my own self back into the bed. The nurses went right back to what they were doing. I just have to say, they better be glad I didn't have the backbone I have today.

The doctor came about fifteen minutes later. He confirmed the miscarriage and sent me up to have a D & C procedure. I did not know what that was because they did not give me one with the first miscarriage. I called Janelle when I knew she was off work. She immediately came to be with me. I had called Erin earlier, but I could not reach him. When Janelle tried, she reached him and told him what happened. He never came to the hospital. Yes, he lived about fifty minutes away, but he didn't even come to see me later. As a matter of fact, I never saw him again. He called one day and told me it was over. So, just like that I lost my baby, and I lost my boyfriend. That was it. I had had enough with men. I always ended up being hurt by men. After that experience, my objective was to be by myself for the rest of my life. Well, that was my plan.

As life continued, I began to believe there had to be more to life. I was just having a hard time finding out what it was. Janelle and I wanted help to deal with the pain from our past. We made an appointment to see a counselor and took Mama along. It literally was a waste of time. Mama didn't want to answer any questions. She didn't want to admit that the abuse happened. She wasn't saying anything until she said, "What did y'all do, just lay there?"

OMG! Janelle and I could not believe what we

heard come out of her mouth. We didn't have the desire to go back, and we never did. Besides, the counselor seemed generic.

I had become dispirited about the miscarriage and breakup for a while, but once again I overcame. I still wondered if I was ever going to have anything to call my own. I had been on the third shift for a few months, and I was offered the opportunity to move to the first shift. I thought it was going to be a wonderful move, but I absolutely hated it!

"May I please, please go back on the third shift?" I begged the supervisor.

"Are you sure you want to move back? You will lose your seniority."

"I don't care. I hate this shift!"

I proudly gave up my seniority and returned to third. People couldn't believe I made that move, but I didn't care. I hated first. Besides, God knew what He had in store for me. Stay tuned.

Romans 8:37 King James Version
Nay, in all these things we are more than conquerors through Him that loved us.

Chapter 7
It Is Well With My Soul

Jeremiah 29:11 New Living Translation
For I know the plans I have for you, says the LORD. They are plans for good and not for disaster, to give you a future and a hope.

I was back on the third shift and as happy as a clam. I was assigned to work with my cousin, Sonia. Sonia's grandma and Grandma Dorothea were sisters. Sonia and I talked about family, and I shared with her the things that I had been through. Our bond grew stronger. We were cousins, but we bonded as close friends. We worked well together because she was a hard and diligent worker, just like me. We raked in a considerable sum of money because we were just that good. It hadn't been that long since I had broken up with Erin. A coworker kept trying to set me up on a date with another worker. He was quiet and seemed like a great guy, but I wasn't interested in him. "I don't want to go out with that young guy!" He was just a year younger than Tyler. It wasn't just that he was younger, it was that I really had made up my mind I wasn't going on any more dates. I was plum fed up with guys.

"Neil really wants to go out with you!" my coworker said.

"Please leave me alone!" I exclaimed.

Ever once and a while, Neil passed by my worktable and gave me a bashful grin. I barely returned the smile, if I gave anything at all. Hours later, my co-worker came back to my table.

"Come on, Sharon. Neil really wants to go out with you."

Tired of her badgering me, I said, "If I say yes, will you then leave me alone?"

"Yes!" she said. "I will send him over here so y'all can exchange information."

"What have I got myself into?" I asked myself.

Neil approached my worktable, and with an attitude I gave him my information. Even though I was uncordial toward him, he still looked overjoyed just to have my information. For me, this was a "yes" to get my coworker to stop nagging me. Neil called me later and we made plans to go out that Friday.

Our first date was on Friday, December 13, 1991. Neil was very punctual when he picked me up, but I purposely took my time getting dressed. I wasn't even ready when he arrived.

"You can come in. I have to finish getting dressed."

Neil waited patiently as I proceeded to get dressed. I was truly dreading this date; however I finally finished dressing and we headed out the door.

"Let me get that for you," Neil offered.

Why was this guy opening my door? I can open my own door, I thought, with an attitude. That was weird. I had never seen that. Besides telling Neil where I wanted to eat, I did not carry on a conversation with him in the car on our way to the restaurant. We were seated in the restaurant and having a quiet meal. I had no shame in eating in front of him. Shoot, I was hungry. Neil had finished with his meal and was patiently waiting until I finished. I was a big eater, but I also was a slow eater. I noticed he still had shrimp on his plate.

"Are you going to eat those shrimp?" I shamelessly asked.

When he shook his head, I reached over and politely grabbed the shrimp from his plate and transferred them to mine. I resumed eating and began to feel guilty. Man, now I have to talk to him. I can't just take his food and not talk to him. I initiated a conversation. I was genuinely very impressed at the way he listened to my every word and how he responded with much interest. That gave me the desire to find out more about him. I wanted to know what he was all about. We continued our date by going to the movies. Unlike the ride to the restaurant, there was a substantial amount of conversation on our way to the movie theater. Neil was bashful, yet conversational. He was very attentive, thoughtful, and much more. I couldn't believe how he captured my heart on this first date. Just think, had I not taken those shrimp, who knows how this date would have ended.

After Neil drove me home, we finished up the date by sitting in his car talking for hours before he left for home. Obviously, we became a couple. It's mind-blowing how God used our coworker to bring us together. We later found out that she had told Neil I was interested in him, just as she straightforwardly told me he was interested in me. Be that as it may, I am just glad it happened. The devil wanted to stop the plan of action God had for me by holding the breakup with Erin over my head. He knew Neil was right around the corner. Nevertheless, our relationship grew stronger and stronger. I was very grateful that Neil was in my life. I needed someone like him.

My life slowly began to change for the better. Even so, there were still times when I tried to push Neil aside. I was having trouble accepting his love for me. How can he love me like this, I wondered. The devil unceasingly tried his best to convince me that the love was not real. He played over and over in my head, "He doesn't want you, Sharon. He's just playing you." Everything that had gone on in my life almost made me believe that lie, but one way or another, Neil always did something distinct to prove to me that the love was real. I never told him about my doubts.

The time had come for me to meet Neil's mama, Roxie. Neil brought me to his grandma's house, and I met his mama, grandma, and stepdad. They were very friendly and welcoming. I felt comfortable around them. The only problem was, I was pregnant, but they didn't know. I kept telling Neil that he needed to tell his mama, but he was nervous. When Roxie learned of my pregnancy, I'm sure she was a little disappointed. But, I think she was more excited than anything. She began sewing baby clothes, blankets, bibs, robes, and so much more for her soon-to-be granddaughter and for me! Roxie was a superb seamstress and she saved us a lot of money.

A Bona Fide Conqueror

After I made it past the first trimester, I was relieved and very thankful. My hope of being able to carry the baby full term greatly increased. Neil's support was encouraging and invigorating. He did not ask me if I wanted to terminate the pregnancy, nor did he act as if it was the worst thing that could've happened to him. He stayed right there by my side the whole nine months.

The time had come. It was time for me to give birth to my baby girl. Since Neil was working third shift and Roxie lived in a different state, I made the decision to stay with my parents while Neil went to work at night. Neil took me to my parents' every night just before he went to work. We felt this was probably better than me being home alone. This was my parents' grandchild, and I felt they had a right to be a part of her life.

"I think it's time," I told Mama and Deddy. It was around two in the morning. I immediately called Neil and he arrived at my parents' house lickety split! My contractions were about ten minutes apart. The hospital was forty-five minutes away, so I didn't want to wait too long before leaving. We loaded up in the car and headed to the hospital. The contractions were getting closer and closer. Every time I screamed out, Deddy stepped on the pedal a little harder.

My total labor was about four and a half hours. I brought my six-pound, four-ounce baby girl into this world on Wednesday, December 16, 1992 at 7:26 am. My first blessing! I named her Briana. It is a popular name now, but back then it was unique. Neil rushed to call our workplace to let them know I had just given birth to a beautiful, baby girl. Neil was so proud to be a dad. It showed on his face. I knew at that moment that he was going to be a wonderful dad.

The used car I had bought was good to me, but it had taken all it could. Neil had a black Fifth Avenue, but he had recently been involved in a wreck and totaled the car. He drove a yellow Volkswagen Beetle which did not have seat belts to fasten in the baby's car seat. Roxie had made plans to take us home from the hospital the next morning, but since I was released a day I needed to find a way home.

Ring Ring.

"Mama, they are releasing me today. Can you come pick me up, please?"

"Girl, I don't want to come back up there."

I kept trying to sway Mama to come pick me up, but it was a lost cause.

Ring Ring.

"Hello," answered Roxie.

"Hello. They are releasing me today. We don't have a way home from the hospital."

"Don't worry. I'll be there. I'm leaving now."
Just like that, I didn't have to beg or plead. Roxie came just like that. She was on her job, not to mention the hospital was two hours away from her. I was in total awe. I will always remember that kind gesture.

Briana brought so much joy to everybody, especially me. Yes, I had Neil, but this was a kind of love that I never felt before. I finally had something I could call my own. As months rolled by, I began to have a difficult time sharing my time between Neil and Briana. I wanted to give all my time to Briana.

A Bona Fide Conqueror

The devil threw something in my face that he thought would break up what God had put together. The Bible says in Mark 10:9, *"What therefore God hath joined together, let no man put asunder."* We may not have completely done things the way God intended us to do them, but I truly believe He ordained our union.

I decided to start attending church again. The church I started attending was Neil's family church, and it's the church where I'm a current member. God had blessed me with a great boyfriend and a precious baby. I couldn't forget about God like I previously tried to. I asked God if it was His will for me to be married to Neil to let him ask me. Long story short, we were married a few weeks after I made that request. I finally felt like I belonged.

Our little family started out blessed and continues to be blessed today. Minus a few years, God has blessed us to be able to take at least one couple's trip or a family's trip each year. I was never able to experience this as a child. Isaiah 61:7 tells me, *"Instead of shame and dishonor, you will inherit a double portion of prosperity and everlasting joy."* This is simply letting me know that God is making up for all the hurt I have experienced in my lift. A lot of things that happened in my life are unexplainable, but I know it is nobody but God and no one can make me think otherwise.

When Briana turned one year old, we gave her a first birthday party. I was elated because I never experienced having a birthday party. I didn't know she was supposed to get messy with the cake, but as prissy as she is she would not have liked that. Well, she probably picked that up from me.

Since I never had a birthday party, even as an adult, I decided to give myself a Fabulous 50th Birthday Bash. It was a Hollywood Glam Party that was so amazing! I will forever hold that exuberant memory close to my heart. Kudos to Neil for letting me obtain whatever I needed for that over-the-top party. I love you, Baby!

To keep the love flowing smoothly, I made sure I kept my time divided between Neil and Briana so that neither one of them felt neglected. All the past trauma in my life made it a little hard, but I was determined. I wanted everyone to be happy. I certainly didn't want to lose Neil.

Because of the balance the love grew stronger and stronger. We soon had a house built and Neil made a job switch, which brought in more money for the family. Yes, things continued looking up for me, but had all my problems disappeared? Nope. When the excitement, not the love, but the excitement started to dwindle down, my past had come back to haunt me. I was married with a beautiful, baby girl. I loved my husband and my daughter with all my heart, but I still found myself depressed and broken-hearted at times. Usually when I thought about the abuse and the neglect in my life, it would cause me to become resentful. I gave Briana the love I never received as a child and the neglect inspired me to give her more love. However, it also caused me to feel unsettled. I was unsettled because I didn't get to experience a love like this, and I wanted to feel that type of love. Yes, I was a young adult, but I still longed for a mother's love.

A Bona Fide Conqueror

Still adjusting to things and trying to escape from my past, I put Neil through the test. It truly let me know he loved me, and I was blessed to have him. I mean, I knew that he loved me, but he proved that it was a selfless love. During our intimate times, if an intrusive thought came in my mind, I fought Neil. The fights weren't as strenuous as the ones with Deddy, but I fought him. Neil would just wrap his arms around me and hold me until I calmed down. If he touched me in a way that reminded me of how Deddy used to touch me, it caused me to freak out. Sometimes I would ball up in a corner. Sometimes I would zone out. It was almost like I went back to that secret place in my head. Neil knew when I was zoned out, but he just held me until I came back. Neil had to experience a lot with me, but he stayed right by my side.

A little over three years later, I became pregnant with our second child. This pregnancy put me through the wringer. I stayed sick practically the entire nine months. One day, my back was hurting so badly. I was desperate for some relief. It came to my mind that Mama had a heating pad.

Ring Ring.

"Hello," Mama answered.

"Mama, will you please, please bring your heating pad? I am in so much pain!"

"Girl, I just got back in the house and I wasn't planning on coming back out. I just put gas in my car."

"Mama, I will give you some gas money. I just need your heating pad. Please!" I begged.

"Nah. I'm not coming out."

I stretched out on the floor until Neil came home from work. I know what you're thinking. Money *ain't* everything, but I can assure you, that's not what it was about. I knew if I had called him, he would have been there right away. But, he is a man who does not like missing work, and I didn't want to mess that up for him. When Neil returned home, he took me straight to the hospital. I ended up being admitted because I had a kidney infection.

Ring Ring.

"Hello," Mama answered.

"I just wanted you to know that I was admitted to the hospital because I have a kidney infection."

It was things like this that Mama did that made it hard for me to understand. I had to finally accept things the way they were. I know for a fact that Mama used to try to tarnish Janelle's and my name. She told people that we wouldn't come to see her or bring the grandchildren to see her. When Briana was younger, I took her to see Mama, and of course, I would be very vigilant. I took her because this was Briana's grandma. I wanted them to have a bond. To be truthful, I didn't worry about her having a bond with her granddad. When we were there, just like Mama didn't give me any attention, she did not give my baby any attention. I brought it up to her one day while I was there, but it didn't change. I got tired of trying, so I stopped going. I really tried, but it made me mad because it reminded me of my childhood. One day I had a discussion with Mama about her filling people's heads with half-truths.

A Bona Fide Conqueror

"Mama, I know you've told people we don't come see you."

Mama said, "No, I haven't told anyone that."

"Mama, yes you have."

After I named some people she said it to and reminded her of what she said, she admitted to it.

"Did you tell them the reasons we don't come?"

Mama never ceases to amaze me.

"I'm not going to tell them that," she said.

"Well Mama, if you're not going to tell them that, then you shouldn't tell them anything at all! Do you realize how that makes us look?"

I love my parents, I really do, but they used to, and I hope they are not still doing it, purposely talk down on us to take the heat off them. Some people believed it and some didn't. It used to bother me, but now it doesn't. That's called growth.

On Monday, December 2, 1996 at 10:09 am, I welcomed my six-pound, fourteen-ounce handsome baby boy into the world. My second blessing! My labor was approximately two and a half hours. My son was coming so fast that the nurses didn't even have time to connect all the wires to me! My doctor said, "Next time, you will need to get to the hospital the first time you have a contraction!" Well, we had no worries there.

Still going to church trying to find restoration, I had to repent for straying away and being angry at God. I found myself growing in Him to a certain extent, but I knew there was still much more to overcome.

About ten years after I moved away from my

parents' home, God told me to go to Deddy and ask him for forgiveness for hating him. Being the person I am, I tried to argue with God and explain to him, "Oh no! If anybody needs to be coming to anybody it's him!" God then told me for my healing to begin, I had to do this. I swallowed my pride and did what was asked. When I arrived at my parents' house, Deddy was there alone. I began to get nervous, but God gave me the strength.

"Hey, how are you," I asked.

Deddy looked around with concern to figure out why I was there.

"I'm good, and you?" We had a brief conversation, and I went straight to the assignment.

"God sent me here to ask you for your forgiveness for hating you. Will you forgive me?"

While waiting on his answer, I saw a tear roll down his cheek. It seemed as if he was trying to hold it back. He sat rigidly with that same somber expression he had back then. Deddy nodded his head but didn't say a word.

"Well, I did what I was supposed to. I'll talk to you later."

I didn't know what he was thinking, so I left right afterwards. It didn't happen all at once, but I felt a little lighter. I had to go through a *mourning* process before the actual *healing* process. This was where I released most of the hurt. I had to weep. I had to grieve. I had to accept.

More changes began to take place. God sent me to a Christian counselor. Mama Lois had the opportunity to come with me to one of the sessions. My counselor let me know that I was blessed to have her in my life. Of course, I already knew that. My counselor knew that Mama Lois was in my life, but she also knew I had limited availability to her.

She asked me one day, "I want to know, how did you make it?

At first, I looked at her like, "Wait a minute, aren't you the counselor?"

I understood where she was coming from. I thought about it for a few seconds, then I said, "God!"

Keep in mind that this was a Christian counselor, so she knew all about God and how He works.

"I understand that," she said. "I have had many cases like yours, but they usually have someone. But you, you had no one. So, again, how did you make it?"

I pondered the question a little longer, then I realized that it had to be nobody but God! Although I didn't think He was there for me, He was there holding me and keeping me sane. The first time when I answered it was God, I basically was just reciting something that I heard other people say all my life. I was saying it without really believing it. When I really thought about it, it registered. So, my answer to her again was, "God!" I said it with more confidence that time.

The counselor then said, "I want you to know that you are a strong, strong person."

After she said that, another revelation was revealed to me. I realized in that moment that I was a strong person. Without knowing it, I had a warrior mindset. I always fought Deddy because I knew what he was doing was wrong. Although I was a young, brainwashed individual, I held on to the hope of getting out of that situation. I was mentally strong! If I had mental strength and willpower to fight against what I was faced with, I was strong! I may have felt weak, LORD knows I did, but He gave me the strength I needed to make it. I did not understand why I had to go through all the hell I went through, but God knew I could handle it. When the devil wanted me to throw my hands up as a sign of giving up, God had been adjusting things perfectly for His glory and for my good.

Some may think they cannot make it through the abuse or think that they can't be delivered from the abuse, but I am a living testimony, YOU CAN MAKE IT! Trust in God. Have the mental strength and the willpower, and you will eventually see that you will make it out. I can't say how or when your story will end, but you must know and believe that God has a plan to turn your pain into purpose. Also, remember you must forgive. That is what will give you peace to go on with your life. I had to forgive Mama, Deddy, my brothers and anyone else who abused me in life. Again, trust God, have mental strength, have willpower and forgive. If you do this, you will surely find yourself as a BONA FIDE CONQUEROR!!!

I am "living my life like it's golden" as I am continuously growing in him. He is showing me how to endure and how to have patience with Him. I'm finding out that everything is not going to happen at once. It's a process. I'm learning to listen to Him more.

A Bona Fide Conqueror

One of the most recent listening experiences with God was when he told me to do something for Mama. Mama had an accident and wanted me to come clean her up. I was refusing to do this task. If we had a better relationship, it probably would not have been as difficult for me. When I hung up the phone, the Holy Spirit told me to go. Once again, I tried to get out of it, but the Holy Spirit kept nudging me. I had recently made a vow to God that I would start doing everything that He asked of me. This was a test. I made a conscious effort to do the task. While I was in the process of the task, I had a worthwhile conversation with Mama.

"Mama, how did it make you feel when I said I wasn't coming?"

"It made me sad. I broke down," Mama whimpered.

"It wasn't a good feeling, was it? I want you to think about that pain you felt. The pain you felt was close to the pain I felt when I needed you."

Mama chimed in, "Mhmm."

"You needed me and I'm here. You never were there for me, but I'm here. I said I wasn't coming, but I'm here."

Mama responded, "Yeah, you are and I appreciate it."

"Mama, I really needed you."

There was much more I released that day, but I just wanted to give the gist of the story. God had me there so I could release things I'd been harboring for so long. I attempted many times to discuss with Mama the things we talked about, but she always deviated from the topics. God let me know that He put Mama in a vulnerable position to hearken to what I had to say. I am thankful that I listened to the Holy Spirit because I left feeling a lot lighter. I may not have the best connection with my parents, but I love them and I have forgiven them. I call to check on them from time to time, and I pray that all is well with the LORD.

God told me the devil had put ample obstacles in my path trying to stop the great plan that He has for my life. With the lack of family stability and the rooted guilt and shame, it was easy for the devil to put voices in my head. He made me feel incompetent and weak. I didn't know the value of life, and the devil made me feel I had no value. When God reminded me who I am and whose I am, my eyes were opened. It took me a while to get where I am today, but God waited for me.

It is never too late. I am no longer "just settling," I am declaring and decreeing everything that God has for me. I vow to do the things it is that the LORD wants me to do. Writing this book is one of them. The abuse and neglect I had to endure was not for me. It is to give others HOPE by sharing my testimony. Isaiah 46:10 in the New Living Translation says, *"Only I can tell you what is going to happen even before it happens. Everything I plan will come to pass, for I do whatever I wish."*

God doesn't want me to dwell in my past, but He does want me to remember it. He wants me to be grateful for the things that He has done and brought me out of. God knew all along that I was going to be victorious. I just had to believe that I was a conqueror, and it was a must for me to put it ALL in His hand. I had to learn how to fight the battle His way instead of my own. I'm not talking about when I was going through the abuse as a child, per se. I had to put it ALL in His hand and fight His way when I was broken as an adult and didn't know what to do. God reminded me that I didn't lose my mind. He kept me. He reminded me that I didn't consume drugs to cope with the pain. He kept me. He reminded me although I was promiscuous, He didn't allow me to fall victim to a sexually transmitted disease. He kept me. God kept me from so much. God told me that He is in it for the long run. He kept me then and He is the one Who is keeping me now. God is going to do exactly what He set out to do in my life. God is fighting for me and with me, so I have nothing to fret. You too have nothing to fret if you give it ALL to God. Remember, if I can make it, so can you. May God bless and keep you.

Romans 8:28 New Living Translation
And we know that God causes everything to work together for the good of those who love God and are called according to His purpose for them.

Acknowledgements

I give God thanks for granting me the strength and determination to write this book. My life is not being exposed for amusement or to assassinate anyone's character. The purpose of writing this book is to give people who have been abused HOPE. God loves you, the broken. He is with you, even when it doesn't feel like it. God patiently waited for me, and He is patiently waiting on You. Give it ALL to God so that you may gain hope and be restored. You are a BONA FIDE CONQUEROR!

The front cover was given to me by God. The laurel wreath is a symbol of triumph. The butterflies symbolize transformation. There are four butterflies altogether (two on the front and two on the back). God dropped the number four in my spirit, and four symbolizes stability and strength. Red is my favorite color and red symbolizes courage and power.

My dear husband Neil, I love you with everything in me. I appreciate that God gave me a man who walks with me, protects me and gives me all his love. Thank you for always believing in me and giving me your support for anything I decide to do. I love you for a lifetime.

My daughter Briana, from the moment I told you that

I was writing this book you believed in me. Thanks for being the wonderful daughter that you are. I believe in you just as much as you believe in me. I love you.

My son Dion, thank you for your support. Thank you for doing the things I needed you to do for this book. I can always count on you. I am so proud to call you my son. I will always believe in you. I love you.

To Serita Acker, I am so glad God allowed you to sow the seed into my life. Thank you for your encouragement and your friendship. I love you.

Marilyn Johnson, thank you for being there when I need you. Our friendship means a lot to me. I love you.

Lynn Smith, thank you so much for your encouragement and the help you provided to me in writing this book. I love you.

Sherry Goodine Catchings, one of my favorite cousins, thank you for being there for me and listening to me. I love you.

Charmian Hanvey, we don't know what God is up to, but I am grateful to have you in my life. I love you.

Cynthia Bibb, we've been through a lot together and it's a privilege to call you my friend. I love you.

A Bona Fide Conqueror

Lula Simmons, we've been friends for a while, and I can still count on you. Thanks for your friendship. I love you.

Roxie Lawrence, you have always been there for me and treat me with great respect, making it easy for me to do the same for you. I love you.

Luellen Gray, you are a woman who would do anything for anybody. Thank you for the love. I love you.

Andrea Cleveland, you have such a sweet spirit. Thank you for being a great sister-in-law. I love you.

Mrs. Louise Wilson, I love you with all my heart. Thank you for being there for me and thank you for being a part of my life.

Tosha McMillian, we have discussed a lot of things. Thank you for listening to me share my dreams, my friend. It only gets better from here. I love you.

Sharon Lewis, I am grateful that God put us together. He knows the plan He has for US. Be encouraged. I love you.

Pastor Hill and First Lady Louise Hill, thank you for being strong leaders. It's an honor to be under your leadership. May God continue to bless you. I love you.

To my entire family, we are family, and we must continue to let the love grow. I love each of you and pray you will make every effort to achieve your dream.

To all my friends, thank you for being in my life. I do not take friendship lightly and it's a blessing to be able to call you, my friend. I will continue wishing the best for each of you. I love you.

Dr. Sonia Leverette and Hadassah's Crown Publishing, LLC, thank you for your willingness and dedication to publish my book. Thank you for your patience and your help to get it published in the time frame I desired. May God continue to bless your business.

To all the people who are being or have been sexually abused and feel like there is no hope, I wrote this book to let you know that you are not alone. There's a fight in you. There is HOPE if you just keep trusting and believing. Just know that you are truly a BONA FIDE CONQUEROR!!!

About the Author

Sharon Quarles is a God-fearing woman. She loves to travel to see the beautiful world created by her Heavenly Father. She has been married for twenty-seven wonderful years. She has a daughter named Briana, who is her oldest child, and a son named Dion. She loves to cook, and she lets God direct her to share her passion. Sharon knows it was NOBODY but God who kept her and brought her to where she is today. And for that, she always smiles.

HadassahsCrownPublishing.com
Publishing Excellence with Integrity

Made in the USA
Columbia, SC
22 June 2021